VEGETARIAN COOKING
OF THE
MEDITERRANEAN

FROM GIBRALTAR TO ISTANBUL

by Cornelia Schinharl

Photography by Heinz-Josef Beckers and Franz Schotten, Jr.

BARRON'S

TABLE OF CONTENTS

The Mediterranean Experience—
Enjoy It with All Your Senses!

Shimmering heat, brilliant colors, sun, shore, and love of life—the Mediterranean countries have them all in excess. This wondrous environment encourages a lush and varied plant growth that in turn produces countless delicacies for vegetarian cuisine.

Of course, the people of the Mediterranean do not eat vegetables alone. Meat and especially seafood are also eaten with pleasure, and as a rule, very simply prepared, such as grilled or broiled. But salads and vegetables are gaining importance. There are few foods that can be prepared in so many new and imaginative ways.

The Mediterranean cuisine not only is varied, creative, and a feast for the senses, but it also boasts healthful benefits that are disputed by none. The blood-cleansing properties of flavor-rich olive oil, and the curative promises of pungent garlic are just two reasons the cuisine is so highly praised among nutrition experts. A diet rich in lean meats, seafood, and fresh vegetables, along with active lifestyles work together to give the Mediterranean people a safeguard against heart disease.

Mediterranean Classics and Novelties
In this book, you'll find dishes from Spain, Italy, Greece, Turkey, and southern France. We haven't included the Mediterranean countries along the northern coast of Africa because that would have exceeded the framework of the book, for Arabic cooking is an exciting subject in itself.

So try the true Mediterranean classics, such as Tzatziki, Tagliatelle with Pesto, Ratatouille, and Potato Omelet, as well as new and unusual combinations, such as Gnocchi with Herb-Saffron Butter or Moussaka, which is prepared here with a spicy onion-nut sauce. In addition, we've listed typical Mediterranean ingredients and their merits on the inside back cover.

4

Eating Vegetarian Is Healthy and Enjoyable

Anyone who eats little or no meat, and eggs only rarely, is simply living more healthfully, as countless dietary studies show. The person whose meals consist mainly of vegetables, salads, legumes, grains, and potatoes consumes less fat and animal protein, and, therefore takes in more vitamins, minerals, and the all-important fiber. You will enjoy preparing and eating the healthy vegetarian creations in this cookbook.

Whole-wheat or White Flour

Eating vegetarian does not mean you must use only super-nutritious ingredients. You also can eat pasta made from white flour, if it tastes better to you. Enjoyment and delight in eating are an intrinsic aspect of physical and emotional well-being. It may take a while until you find a kind of pasta or rice that you really like. Try various products—the choices these days are numerous!

Decide whether to use white or whole-wheat flour, or compromise and use a blend. There is little difference when making dough; you may have to add a little more water with whole-wheat flour. Instead of wheat, you can also use spelt flour, which is available in health-food stores. Spelt has an unusual type of gluten with higher water solubility for easier digestibility than gluten in other wheats. Its baking qualities are better, but it also is more expensive.

Another Way to Sweeten

For sweet foods, instead of refined white sugar, you can use brown sugar or even maple syrup, if you want to give the dessert a special flavor. More important than the choice of sweetener is the quantity; sweeten as little as possible!

Bio-logical

When shopping, pay attention to where the products originate and how they are grown. The offerings of organically grown products have become so large that you can get high-quality vegetables, grains, and milk products almost anywhere. Just as important as the growing method is the freshness of the product. The shorter the transportation time, the fresher the goods. Therefore, give preference to the vegetables in season in your area. Buy carefully, and find out where the products come from. You'll notice that they will taste better.

Special Note

The recipes in this cookbook list salt as an ingredient, with no quantity given. This way, the cook can salt to taste. The salt quantity used to create the nutritional charts for each recipe is $1/8$ teaspoon.

Off to a Colorful
Start

Appetizers

What would Mediterranean cuisine be without appetizers—those diverse, delicious offerings of spicy little things prepared with flavorful sun-ripened ingredients, sometimes stuffed, sometimes marinated, sometimes roasted, or served as salad?

Quality, Quality

Important for the preparation of appetizers—and, of course, for the other dishes in this book—is the quality of the vegetables, which are the chief ingredients in most Mediterranean specialties. The vegetables you choose may indeed be perfectly symmetrical and unblemished, but if they are watery, the most ingeniously devised recipe will be transformed into a tasteless dish. Therefore, it pays to look for a vegetable dealer, a stand at the market, or a natural-food store that offers fully ripened vegetables of good quality. Produce managers in the smaller stores, after a while, will get to know you, and you can ask where the vegetables come from, or let them know if you weren't entirely pleased with them. Likewise, it's advantageous to choose produce in season. This is borne out in taste as well as in price. The seasonal calendar on the inside front cover will help you determine when the vegetables and fruits are at their peaks.

Good Combinations

Choose a single appetizer or, even better, offer a small choice of mixed appetizers. Your guests will be very pleased, for many people would rather eat three appetizers than one main dish.

Appetizers that go well together are

- Tzatziki (page 12), Zucchini Fritters (page 15), and Broiled Peppers with Feta Cheese (page 10)

- Tomato Crostini (page 10), Orange Salad with Black Olives (page 19), and Marinated Zucchini (page 17)

- Carrot Yogurt (page 12), Bulgur Salad (page 25), and Eggplant Tartare (page 20)

- Stuffed Tomatoes (page 15), Marinated Onions (page 17), and White Bean Salad (page 22)

Colorful Buffets

Likewise, everyone loves colorful appetizer buffets. For twenty people, pick out about ten recipes and prepare double quantities of each one. These can be stretched with bread and cheese, and, if you like, ham or salami. You should offer one or two desserts, as well. Thus, you've put together a delightful meal that can be prepared ahead of time and is sure to be enjoyed by everyone.

If you want to prepare only one dish and still have a large choice of appetizers, you can offer some delicacies from Greek, Turkish, or Italian gourmet shops, such as olives (plain, spicy, or stuffed), marinated artichoke hearts (relatively expensive, but delicious), oil-packed sun-dried tomatoes, and marinated hot peppers.

To Set the Mood: An Apéritif

Your guests will enjoy being greeted with an apéritif and an appetizer. This can be a refreshing glass of Prosecco or champagne—especially welcome on hot summer days—a dry or semidry sherry, a vermouth, or a light mixed drink. Try fresh-squeezed grapefruit juice with some canned coconut milk, cream, and sugar to taste; mix all thoroughly in the blender. Instead of grapefruit juice, pineapple juice also tastes good, but then mix in some lemon juice and omit the sugar. If you want, mix a shot of white rum into the drinks. Also welcome is kir royale (champagne or dry white wine with a shot of cassis) or Campari with orange juice and ice.

Plus . . .

You should always offer plenty of bread. Whether you choose a crusty white or whole-wheat baguette depends on your tastes and those of your guests. Flat bread and pita bread cut in quarters and toasted are also good choices.

Preparations—Easily Made

Almost all appetizers can be prepared ahead of time and stored until time to eat. Cover them with plastic wrap or a plate, and place the appetizers in the refrigerator.

Take them out at least one hour before the guests arrive. All appetizers develop their flavor better at room temperature. If you forget to take them out in time, put them—marinated vegetables especially—into a hot oven for a few minutes!

Tomato Crostini

1 medium-size tomato
6 oil-packed sun-dried tomatoes
1 clove garlic
1/2 bunch basil
2 teaspoons capers
2 tablespoons olive oil
salt
freshly ground black pepper
12 (1/2-inch/1-cm) slices white or whole-wheat French or Italian bread

Preparation time:
About 30 minutes

Broiled Peppers with Feta Cheese

4 small, oblong red bell peppers
1/2 bunch parsley
1 tablespoon fresh lemon juice
salt
freshly ground white pepper
2 tablespoons olive oil
1/2 lb (200 g) firm feta cheese

Preparation time:
About 45 minutes (plus about 1 hour for marinating)

Tomato Crostini
From Italy • Pictured

• Wash the fresh tomato and remove the stem. Dice very fine and place in a large bowl. Dice the dried tomatoes very fine; add to bowl. Peel the garlic, chop fine, and add to tomatoes. Wash the basil and shake it dry. Pull off the leaves and cut into strips; add to tomato mixture.

• Stir in capers and oil, then season to taste with salt and pepper.

• Before serving, brown the bread slices in a 475°F (250°C) oven on a baking sheet for about 4 minutes. Divide the tomato mixture among the slices and serve the crostini immediately. Makes 4 servings.

Variation: Mozzarella Crostini

Chop the fresh and 2 dried tomatoes. Add garlic and basil. Season with salt and pepper, and divide mixture among the untoasted bread slices. Cover each slice with one 1/4-inch thick mozzarella slice. Bake about 5 minutes in a 475°F (250°C) oven.

PER SERVING:	288 CALORIES	
NUTRITIONAL INFORMATION*		
Carbohydrate	42	g
Protein	7	g
Total fat	10	g
Cholesterol	0	mg
Sodium	675	mg
Fiber	2	g

*Refers to original recipe only.

Broiled Peppers with Feta Cheese
From Greece • More time-consuming

• Preheat the oven to 475°F (250°C). Wash the peppers, cut off the tops, and remove the seeds. Place peppers on a baking sheet and bake them for about 20 minutes, or until the skins blister.

• Remove the peppers, cover with a damp cloth, and let them stand briefly. When cool enough to handle, remove the skins.

• Wash the parsley and chop it fine. Place parsley in a medium-size bowl with the lemon juice, salt, and pepper. Beat in the oil. Drizzle this marinade over the insides and outsides of the peppers, then let them stand for at least 1 hour, or overnight.

• Heat the broiler. Cut the feta into 8 equal pieces. Put 2 cheese slices into each pepper. Lay peppers on a rack over a baking sheet, and place them under the broiler. Broil for about 8 minutes, turning them once. Serve warm. Makes 4 servings.

PER SERVING:	235 CALORIES	
NUTRITIONAL INFORMATION		
Carbohydrate	8	g
Protein	9	g
Total fat	19	g
Cholesterol	50	mg
Sodium	716	mg
Fiber	2	g

Tzatziki
From Greece • Classic

• Peel the cucumber and cut it in half lengthwise. Scoop out the seeds with a spoon and grate the halves, or dice them very small. In a small bowl, mix the cucumber and salt; let it sit for about 10 minutes, then pour off the liquid.

• Peel the garlic and put it through a garlic press; add to cucumber. Wash the mint, pat it dry, and cut into strips. Add to the cucumber along with the yogurt. Mix in the lemon juice and oil and season with salt to taste.

• Tzatziki is good along with fresh bread or with other appetizers, such as Zucchini Fritters or Broiled Peppers with Feta Cheese. Makes 4 servings.

Tip

The Turkish make a very similar appetizer. It is prepared with less cucumber and more yogurt.

Carrot Yogurt
From Turkey • Pictured

• Peel the carrots and grate fine; set aside. Peel the garlic and put it through a garlic press; set aside.

• Heat the butter in a sauté pan over medium heat. Add the carrots and heat briefly, stirring, without browning them. Season with salt, and place in a large bowl.

• Wash the dill, shake it dry, and cut it fine, removing the coarse stems. Stir the dill, garlic, and yogurt into the carrots and mix thoroughly. Season with salt and allow to cool. Makes 4 servings.

PER SERVING:	98 CALORIES	
NUTRITIONAL INFORMATION		
Carbohydrate	10	g
Protein	6	g
Total fat	4	g
Cholesterol	2	mg
Sodium	151	mg
Fiber	1	g

PER SERVING:	75 CALORIES	
NUTRITIONAL INFORMATION		
Carbohydrate	8	g
Protein	4	g
Total fat	3	g
Cholesterol	9	mg
Sodium	130	mg
Fiber	1	g

Zucchini Fritters
From Greece • Pictured

• Wash and pat dry the zucchini. Remove and discard stems and flowers, and grate the zucchini. Wrap grated zucchini in a kitchen towel, twist the towel, and press out as much liquid as possible. Peel and grate the onion.

• In a large pan, heat 1 tablespoon oil over high heat. Add zucchini and onion and fry until all liquid has evaporated. Put the fried vegetables in a large mixing bowl.

• Grate or crumble the feta cheese and add to vegetables. Wash the mint and finely chop the leaves; add to the vegetable mixture along with the flour and eggs. Mix thoroughly. Season with salt and pepper, but be careful, the cheese is already salty!

• Heat the remaining oil in a large pan. Place small heaps of the zucchini mixture in the pan and fry over medium heat for about 7 minutes, or until golden brown, then turn, and cook about 3 minutes more. Serve hot or cold. Makes 4 servings.

July 2018 - very yummy! 4/5

Stuffed Tomatoes
From Italy • Classic

• Wash the tomatoes and cut in half horizontally. Scoop out part of the seeds and pulp and reserve for another recipe, if desired. Salt and pepper the tomatoes and place in a baking dish.

• Preheat the oven to 400°F (200°C). Wash the parsley, shake dry, and chop fine, removing the stems. Peel the garlic cloves and put them through a garlic press. In a large bowl, combine the parsley, garlic, cheese, and bread crumbs. Add enough oil to make a cohesive mixture.

• Season the herb-cheese mixture with salt and pepper (be careful; the cheese is salty), and stuff the tomatoes.

• Bake the tomatoes for about 30 minutes, or until browned. Allow to cool. Makes 4 servings.

Zucchini Fritters

2 medium-size (250 g) zucchini

1 medium-size onion

2 tablespoons olive oil, divided

2 oz (50 g) firm feta cheese

4 sprigs fresh mint or dill

1/2 cup (50 g) whole-wheat or spelt flour (see page 5)

2 eggs

salt

freshly ground black pepper

Preparation time: About 45 minutes

Stuffed Tomatoes

8 (550 g) small, firm tomatoes

salt

freshly ground white pepper

1 bunch parsley

1 or 2 cloves garlic

1/2 cup (40 g) freshly grated Parmesan cheese

1/2 cup (40 g) bread crumbs (possibly whole-wheat bread)

1/4 cup (60 ml) olive oil

Preparation time: About 45 minutes

PER SERVING:	209 CALORIES	
NUTRITIONAL INFORMATION		
Carbohydrate	17	g
Protein	8	g
Total fat	13	g
Cholesterol	119	mg
Sodium	267	mg
Fiber	3	g

PER SERVING:	238 CALORIES	
NUTRITIONAL INFORMATION		
Carbohydrate	16	g
Protein	7	g
Total fat	18	g
Cholesterol	8	mg
Sodium	319	mg
Fiber	3	g

15

Marinated Zucchini

From Italy • More time-consuming

• Wash the zucchini and cut into slices about $1/4$ inch ($1/2$ cm) thick; set aside. Wash the lemon in hot water, cut off the peel thinly, and cut into strips; set aside in a large bowl. Squeeze the lemon juice into a small bowl. Peel the garlic and cut into thin slices; add to lemon peel. Wash the parsley and chop it fine; add to lemon peel.

• Heat the oil in a large pan over medium heat a little at a time. Add zucchini in batches and sauté until browned. Remove zucchini with a slotted spoon and place in a large bowl; season with salt.

• Loosen the browned bits in the pan with about 1 tablespoon lemon juice, white wine, and $1/4$ cup (60 ml) water. Stir in the lemon peel, garlic, parsley, capers, salt, and pepper.

• Pour the mixture over the zucchini and allow it to marinate for at least 8 hours, stirring occasionally.

• When ready to serve, briefly immerse the tomato in boiling water, then peel and dice. Scatter the diced tomato over the zucchini and serve. Makes 4 servings.

PER SERVING:	162 CALORIES	
NUTRITIONAL INFORMATION		
Carbohydrate	8	g
Protein	2	g
Total fat	14	g
Cholesterol	0	mg
Sodium	141	mg
Fiber	2	g

Marinated Onions

From Italy • Subtle

• Peel the onions and leave them whole. Wash the thyme and strip the leaves from the stems.

• Heat the oil in a pan. Add the onions and sear, stirring, over medium heat, for about 10 minutes, or until they are brown all over. They should get a nice color but not burn, or they will taste bitter.

• Pour in the wine, vinegar, and $1/2$ cup (100 ml) water. Crumble the chili, then add to the pan along with thyme and bay leaves. Season to taste with salt and pepper, then cook, covered, over medium heat for about 10 minutes or until onions are done but still firm. Keep checking from time to time; don't let them get too soft.

• Put the onions and the broth in a bowl, cover, and let marinate for at least 8 hours at room temperature. Remove the bay leaves. The onions taste best with whole-wheat French or Italian bread. Makes 4 servings.

PER SERVING:	183 CALORIES	
NUTRITIONAL INFORMATION		
Carbohydrate	10	g
Protein	1	g
Total fat	14	g
Cholesterol	0	mg
Sodium	5	mg
Fiber	2	g

Marinated Zucchini

$1^1/4$ lb (600 g) zucchini
$1/2$ lemon
2 or 3 cloves garlic
1 bunch parsley
$1/4$ cup (60 ml) olive oil
salt
scant $1/4$ cup (50 ml) dry white wine or vegetable broth
2 teaspoons capers
freshly ground white pepper
1 tomato, for garnish

Preparation time:
About 45 minutes
(plus about 8 hours for marinating)

Marinated Onions

1 lb (500 g) small onions or shallots
$1/2$ bunch fresh thyme
$1/4$ cup (60 ml) olive oil
$1/2$ cup (100 ml) dry white wine or vegetable broth
1 tablespoon white wine vinegar
1 dried chili
2 bay leaves
salt
freshly ground white pepper

Preparation time:
About 35 minutes
(plus about 8 hours for marinating)

Orange Salad with Black Olives

From Italy • Pictured

• Peel the oranges, being sure to remove the white pith as well. Cut the oranges into thin slices and arrange decoratively on a platter or 4 plates.

• Cut the olives in half and distribute them over the oranges. Wash the rosemary and pat it dry. Strip the needles off the sprigs and chop fine. Sprinkle chopped rosemary over the oranges and season with salt and pepper.

• In a small bowl, beat the vinegar with the oil, then drizzle over the oranges. Serve immediately. Makes 4 servings.

Variations:

Instead of olives, 1 mild white onion sliced into rings also tastes very good. The salad may be enriched with about 3½ oz (100 g) firm ricotta (known as ricotta salata, available in cheese shops) or feta cheese, which you cut into small cubes and sprinkle over the salad.

PER SERVING:	107 CALORIES	
NUTRITIONAL INFORMATION*		
Carbohydrate 16	g
Protein 1	g
Total fat 5	g
Cholesterol 0	mg
Sodium 188	mg
Fiber 3	g

Refers to original recipe only.

Vegetable Salad with Olive Dressing

From France • Subtle

• Wash the potatoes; cook in a covered pan, with enough water to cover, over medium heat for about 20 minutes, or until just tender. When cool enough to handle, peel and cut potatoes into ½-inch- (1-cm) square cubes. Place in a large bowl.

• Meanwhile, peel the onions and blanch in boiling water for about 4 minutes; they should remain firm to the bite. Rinse with cold water and allow to dry thoroughly before adding to potatoes.

• Wash the tomatoes and remove the stems; finely chop tomatoes and add to the bowl. Wash the parsley and chop fine; sprinkle over vegetables in the bowl.

• For the salad dressing, purée the olives, capers, pine nuts, and oil in a food processor. Mix in vinegar, salt, and pepper.

• Carefully mix the dressing with the vegetables, then divide among 4 plates. Garnish the salad with pitted whole black olives and parsley leaves. Makes 4 servings.

PER SERVING:	316 CALORIES	
NUTRITIONAL INFORMATION		
Carbohydrate 39	g
Protein 5	g
Total fat 17	g
Cholesterol 0	mg
Sodium 270	mg
Fiber 5	g

Orange Salad with Black Olives

4 juicy oranges
12 pitted black olives
2 sprigs fresh rosemary
salt
freshly ground black pepper
1 teaspoon white wine vinegar
1 tablespoon olive oil

*Preparation time:
About 15 minutes*

Vegetable Salad

1 lb (400 g) cooking potatoes
½ lb (200 g) small white onions
1 lb (400 g) firm tomatoes
½ bunch parsley

For the salad dressing:
15 pitted black olives
1 tablespoon capers
1 tablespoon pine nuts
¼ cup (60 ml) olive oil
2 tablespoons white wine vinegar
salt
freshly ground black pepper

For garnish:
Olives and parsley leaves

*Preparation time:
About 50 minutes*

Eggplant Tartare

1 medium-size (650 g)
eggplant

1 tomato

1 onion

1 or 2 cloves garlic

1 green bell pepper

3 to 4 tablespoons fresh
lemon juice

2 tablespoons olive oil

salt

large pinch Hungarian
paprika or cayenne pepper

Preparation time:
About 50 minutes (including
35 minutes for baking)

Farmer's Salad

2 beefsteak tomatoes

1 cucumber

1 mild white onion

1 large green bell pepper

fresh mint leaves

1/2 lb (200 g) firm feta
cheese

15 pitted black olives

2 tablespoons fresh lemon
juice or white wine vinegar

salt

freshly ground white pepper

1/4 cup (60 ml) olive oil

1/2 teaspoon dried oregano

Preparation time:
About 20 minutes

Eggplant Tartare
From Turkey • Subtle

• Preheat the oven to 425°F (220°C). Wash and dry the eggplant. Place eggplant on a baking sheet and bake for about 35 minutes, or until it is soft and the skin has turned dark; turn the eggplant once while baking.

• Remove the eggplant and allow to cool somewhat. Cut in half lengthwise, and scoop out the meat with a spoon; cut it up fine and place it in a dish.

• Wash the tomato and remove the stem. Peel the onion and garlic. Wash the pepper and remove the stem and seeds. Cut up these ingredients as fine as possible, and add to chopped eggplant.

• Season with lemon juice, oil, salt, and paprika. Serve immediately, otherwise the tartare will release too much juice. Makes 4 servings.

PER SERVING:	189 CALORIES	
NUTRITIONAL INFORMATION		
Carbohydrate	31	g
Protein	5	g
Total fat	8	g
Cholesterol	0	mg
Sodium	88	mg
Fiber	11	g

Farmer's Salad
From Greece • Pictured

• Wash and dry the tomatoes, removing the stems. Cut tomatoes into small pieces and place them in a large bowl. Wash the cucumber and pat it dry. Halve the cucumber lengthwise, then slice into pieces about 1/4 inch (1/2 cm) thick; add to bowl.

• Peel the onion and slice into fine rings; add to bowl. Wash the pepper and remove the stem and seeds; cut into small strips and add to bowl. Wash the mint, pat it dry, and cut into strips. Dice the feta cheese.

• Add mint, feta, and olives to the bowl. Mix in the lemon juice, salt, pepper, and oil. Toss the salad and adjust seasonings to taste. Divide the salad onto 4 plates and sprinkle each with oregano. Makes 4 servings.

Oct 2020 - 5/5
Made without mint

PER SERVING:	343 CALORIES	
NUTRITIONAL INFORMATION		
Carbohydrate	16	g
Protein	10	g
Total fat	28	g
Cholesterol	50	mg
Sodium	860	mg
Fiber	3	g

White Bean Salad

1 (15-oz/400-g) can cooked cannellini beans

1 mild white onion

1 clove garlic

1 tomato

1 bunch basil

1 to 2 teaspoons capers

2 tablespoons white wine vinegar

salt

freshly ground white pepper

3 tablespoons olive oil

Preparation time:
About 20 minutes

Mashed Potatoes with Garlic

1 lb (300 g) potatoes

2 to 3 cloves garlic

fresh mint, parsley, or dill leaves

2 to 3 tablespoons fresh lemon juice

3 tablespoons olive oil

salt

freshly ground white pepper

For garnish:
Black olives

Preparation time:
About 45 minutes

White Bean Salad
From Italy • Pictured

• Rinse and drain the beans and place them in a large bowl. Peel the onion and garlic; slice the onion into thin rings, and chop the garlic. Add onion and garlic to bowl. Wash the tomato, removing the stem, and dice it fine. Wash the basil, blot the leaves dry, and chop fine. Add tomato and basil to bowl, along with the capers.

• In a small bowl, stir together the vinegar, salt, and pepper. Slowly beat in the oil, a little at a time. Thoroughly mix the dressing with the bean mixture, then season with salt and pepper. Makes 4 servings.

Variation from Greece:
Chop tomatoes, scallions, parsley, and mint. Mix with the beans, then dress with vinegar and olive oil.

Variation from Turkey:
Chop tomatoes, onions, green pepper, and parsley. Mix with the beans, then dress with vinegar, oil, and some tahini (sesame paste).

Mashed Potatoes with Garlic
From Greece • Easy to make

• Wash the potatoes and put them, unpeeled, in a pot with enough water to cover. Cook, covered, over medium heat for 20–30 minutes, or until soft.

• Pour off the water and, when the potatoes have stopped steaming, place them in a large bowl. Peel and mash them fine, with a fork or a potato masher.

• Peel the garlic and put through a press; add to potatoes. Wash the mint, pat it dry, and chop fine; sprinkle over potatoes. Add about 6 tablespoons hot water, lemon juice, and oil to the potatoes, and mix well. It should be a smooth, creamy mixture.

• Season the mashed potatoes to taste with salt, pepper, and lemon juice. Serve garnished with olives. Makes 4 servings.

22

PER SERVING:	261 CALORIES	
NUTRITIONAL INFORMATION*		
Carbohydrate	32	g
Protein	11	g
Total fat	11	g
Cholesterol	0	mg
Sodium	110	mg
Fiber	8	g

*Refers to original recipe only.

PER SERVING:	199 CALORIES	
NUTRITIONAL INFORMATION		
Carbohydrate	25	g
Protein	2	g
Total fat	11	g
Cholesterol	0	mg
Sodium	152	mg
Fiber	2	g

Bulgur Salad
From Turkey • Pictured

• Mix the bulgur in a dish with about 1½ cups (³⁄₈ l) cold water; let soak for about 1 hour, or until it is soft, stirring occasionally so that it becomes evenly moist. The soaking time depends on how fresh the bulgur is.

• Briefly submerge tomatoes in boiling water, then peel. Remove the stems, then chop tomatoes very fine. Wash the scallions, trim them, and chop fine. Remove the seeds from the pepper; wash it, and chop as fine as possible. Wash the herbs, shake them dry, and chop very fine.

• Mix tomatoes, scallions, pepper, and herbs with bulgur. Stir in lemon juice and oil, then season with salt, pepper, and ground caraway. Makes 6 servings.

Tip
Bulgur is cooked, dried, cracked wheat. You can buy it in specialty food stores and some grocery stores.

Hummus
From Turkey • Easy to make

• Place chickpeas in a food processor. Peel the garlic, and add to the processor, along with lemon juice, cumin, and about ¼ cup (60 ml) water. Process until smooth.

• Add the tahini and blend well. Season with salt and paprika to taste. Wash the parsley, shake dry, and chop it fine, leaving out the coarse stems. Put the hummus in a dish and serve sprinkled with parsley and paprika. Serve with pita bread and raw vegetables. Makes 6 servings.

Tips
• Tahini can be purchased in some supermarkets, and Middle Eastern and health-food stores.

• If you like, you can cook the chickpeas yourself. Soften dried peas, about ½ cup (100 g), overnight in cold water, then cook in fresh water, without salt, covered, for about 1 hour.

Bulgur Salad
1 cup (250 g) bulgur

4 tomatoes

1 bunch scallions

1 green bell pepper

½ bunch each: parsley and mint

2 tablespoons fresh lemon juice

3 tablespoons olive oil

salt

freshly ground white pepper

½ teaspoon ground caraway

Preparation time:
About 30 minutes (plus about 1 hour soaking time)

Hummus
8½ oz (240 g) canned chickpeas (rinsed and drained)

2 cloves garlic

juice of ½ lemon

1 teaspoon ground cumin

2 tablespoons tahini (sesame paste)

salt

1 teaspoon Hungarian paprika

1 bunch parsley

For garnish:
Paprika

Preparation time:
About 10 minutes

PER SERVING:	176 CALORIES
NUTRITIONAL INFORMATION	
Carbohydrate	26 g
Protein	4 g
Total fat	8 g
Cholesterol	0 mg
Sodium	66 mg
Fiber	6 g

PER SERVING:	136 CALORIES
NUTRITIONAL INFORMATION	
Carbohydrate	21 g
Protein	6 g
Total fat	4 g
Cholesterol	0 mg
Sodium	525 mg
Fiber	6 g

ONE POT, ONE COVER

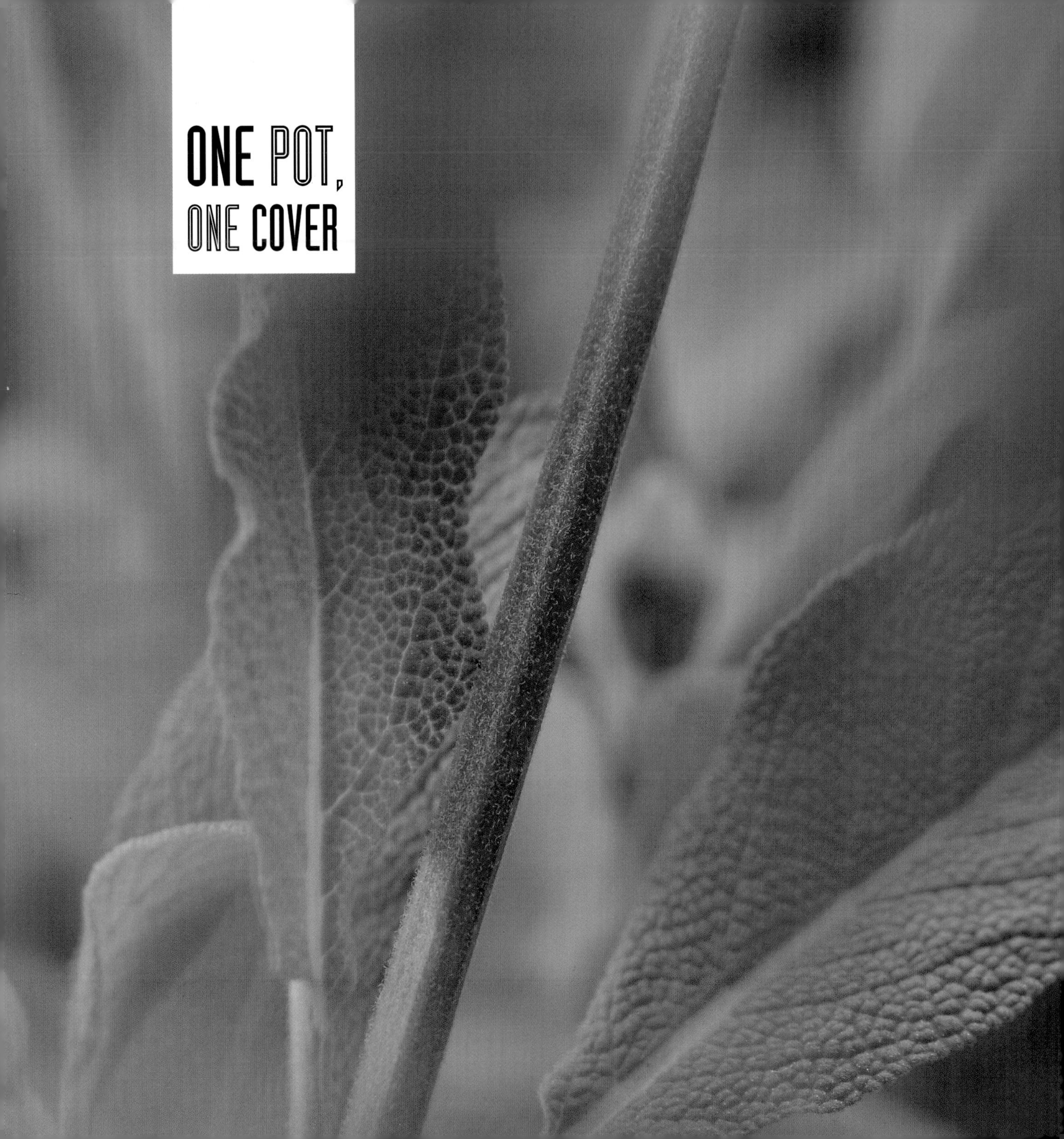

Soups and Stews

A few flavorful vegetables and broth, seasoned with garlic and herbs, can be combined to make an array of the fantastic soups found in the Mediterranean countries. Whether you are looking for a refreshingly cool summer soup or something more warming, the selection in this chapter offers something for every taste. In addition, there are two vegetable stews, which satisfy with their fresh and varied vegetable combinations.

The Cold Vegetable Soup and the Cream of Pumpkin Soup are spicy appetizers; the others are satisfying main dishes. If you offer a dessert or a selection of cheeses, you and your guests will certainly be more than satisfied.

Bouillon Basics

All soups are prepared with water or vegetable broth, which you can make by using the recipe on page 29, or with canned vegetable stock. When using canned stock, use about three fourths of the amount recommended in the recipe. Substitute water for the remaining amount of stock because the canned stock is very concentrated.

Vegetable broth from cubes or granules is strongly seasoned and less suitable, since the seasoning may not complement the dish being prepared.

Anyone who isn't a strict vegetarian can prepare the soups with meat or chicken broth.

What Goes into the Soup?

• Chickpeas are available dried or in cans. Dried chickpeas have to be soaked overnight, then cooked for at least 1 hour; you can find canned chickpeas in the supermarket.

• Red lentils are hulled and, therefore, have a relatively short cooking time. These flavorful legumes do not need to be soaked. You can buy them in health-food stores, specialty supermarkets, or Indian and Middle Eastern groceries.

• Small artichokes that can be eaten whole usually come from California. The fat, fleshy larger globes are not suitable for the vegetable stew. Always remove the outer leaves from the small artichokes, and trim the points off the other leaves with scissors so that the tough portions of the leaves are removed.

• Fava beans (also called broad beans or horse beans) can be purchased dried, frozen, canned, and, infrequently, fresh. Inside the long, broad fresh pods, the beans can be whitish, green, brown, red, or almost black. Usually the green beans are the ones used fresh. Fava beans should never be eaten raw because many people have allergic reactions to them. These beans are available fresh in the markets from May to August.

Vegetable Stock—The Basis of a Good Soup

A delicious soup requires a good stock. To make the stock, trim, wash, and chop fine 3^1/$_3$ lb (1^1/$_2$ kg) mixed vegetables (tomatoes, fennel, celery, leeks, and carrots). Boil the vegetables in 1^1/$_2$ quart (1^1/$_2$ l) water in a large stock pot with parsley, thyme, and fresh bay leaves for 30 minutes. Add a few white peppercorns, cloves, salt, and possibly some juniper berries. Strain and use right away, or freeze in portions. Makes about 2 quarts stock.

Cold Vegetable Soup with Croutons

4 slices toasted bread, divided

1 mild white onion

3 cloves garlic

4 tablespoons olive oil, divided

1¹/₈ lb (500 g) ripe tomatoes

1 medium-size cucumber

1 small red bell pepper

1 small green bell pepper

1 bunch parsley

2 tablespoons red or white wine vinegar

salt

freshly ground white pepper

cayenne pepper

10 pitted black olives

Preparation time:
About 25 minutes (plus about 1 hour for cooling)

Garlic Soup

7 oz (200 g) crustless white bread slices

¹/₂ cup (100 ml) milk

8 cloves garlic

1 red bell pepper

¹/₄ cup (60 ml) olive oil

1 quart (1 l) water

salt

2 eggs

1 small bunch parsley

Preparation time:
About 1 hour

Cold Vegetable Soup with Croutons
From Spain • Pictured

• In a small bowl, soften 2 slices of toast briefly in water. Peel onion and garlic and coarsely chop them.

• Squeeze the water out of the bread and purée in a food processor with onion, garlic, and 2 tablespoons oil. Place mixture in a large bowl.

• Peel tomatoes and dice coarsely. Peel cucumber, cut in half lengthwise, and chop coarsely. Wash bell peppers, remove seeds, and chop coarsely. Wash parsley and chop coarsely.

• Remove about 1 tablespoon each of the cucumber and bell pepper; chop both very fine; set aside. Add parsley and remaining vegetables to the processor and chop fine. Thin with about ¹/₂ cup (100 ml) water, then stir into bread purée. Season with vinegar, salt, white pepper, and cayenne. Mix in 1 tablespoon oil.

• Cut remaining toast into cubes and sauté it golden brown in the last tablespoon of oil. Let cool. Dice the olives. Serve soup garnished with olives, reserved vegetables, and croutons. Makes 6 servings.

PER SERVING:	189 CALORIES	
NUTRITIONAL INFORMATION		
Carbohydrate	21	g
Protein	4	g
Total fat	11	g
Cholesterol	0	mg
Sodium	291	mg
Fiber	5	g

Garlic Soup
From Spain • Easy to make

• In a small bowl, soften bread in milk several minutes. Squeeze out milk, crumbling bread; set aside. Peel the garlic and chop fine. Wash and seed pepper, then chop fine.

• Heat oil in a soup pot over medium heat. Add garlic and bell pepper and brown, stirring constantly. Add bread crumbs and brown a little longer.

• Add water, then season with salt. Let simmer, covered, over medium heat for 20 minutes.

• Carefully transfer soup to food processor or blender, and process to purée. This will need to be done in batches. Return purée to soup pot, off the stove. In a small bowl, whisk the eggs slightly. Wash the parsley and chop fine; set aside.

• Whisk eggs into purée. Briefly warm soup, but do not let it boil. Sprinkle with parsley and serve. Makes 6 servings.

PER SERVING:	298 CALORIES	
NUTRITIONAL INFORMATION		
Carbohydrate	25	g
Protein	8	g
Total fat	18	g
Cholesterol	108	mg
Sodium	336	mg
Fiber	2	g

Vegetable Soup with Basil Purée

From France • Perfect for company

• Peel garlic and mash through a press into a blender. Wash the basil and shake it dry. Pull off the leaves and chop fine. Add basil and oil to blender and process to purée. Season the purée with salt and pepper. Set aside.

• Peel and seed squash; cut squash flesh into small dice.

• Wash the beans. Trim, removing any strings, and cut into pieces about 3/4 inch (2 cm) long.

• Briefly immerse tomatoes in boiling water. Rinse with cold water, then peel, removing stems. Cut tomatoes into small dice.

• Peel the carrots and potatoes and cut into small cubes.

• Wash the scallions. Trim, then slice them fine, including the green tops.

• Place chopped vegetables and peas in a large pot with 1 1/2 quarts (1 1/2 l) water over high heat; bring to a boil. Season with salt and pepper. Add thyme sprigs and bay leaves. Cook, covered, over medium heat for about 25 minutes, until vegetables are just firm to the bite. Stir occasionally, and add more water as necessary.

• Add the macaroni to soup; let cook for about 10 minutes or until pasta is *al dente*. Remove thyme and bay leaves from the soup.

• Divide soup among 6 warm bowls. Garnish each with basil purée and grated cheese and serve immediately. Serve with fresh whole-wheat French or Italian bread. Makes 6 servings.

4 cloves garlic

2 bunches basil

1/4 cup (60 ml) olive oil

salt

freshly ground white pepper

1 1/2 lb (700 g) winter squash

1 lb (500 g) green beans

1/2 lb (200 g) tomatoes

4 carrots

2 cooking potatoes

1 bunch scallions

1/2 cup (100 g) shelled peas, fresh or frozen

1 1/2 quarts (1 1/2 l) water

2 or 3 sprigs fresh thyme

2 fresh or dried bay leaves

1/4 lb (100 g) large elbow macaroni

1/4 cup (50 g) Pecorino cheese, freshly grated

Preparation time: About 1 1/4 hours

PER SERVING:	319 CALORIES
NUTRITIONAL INFORMATION	
Carbohydrate 49	g
Protein 10	g
Total fat 11	g
Cholesterol 3	mg
Sodium 143	mg
Fiber 8	g

Chickpea Soup with Spinach

1/2 lb (250 g) dried chickpeas

2 onions

2 cloves garlic

1 small carrot

1 stalk celery

1 leek

1/4 cup (60 ml) olive oil

5 cups (1 1/4 l) vegetable
stock (see page 29)

1/2 lb (250 g) fresh spinach

1 bunch parsley

salt

freshly ground white pepper

3 to 4 tablespoons fresh
lemon juice

Preparation time:
About 1 1/2 hours (plus about
12 hours for soaking)

Bread Soup with Mozzarella

8 slices (250 g) white or
coarse brown bread

1/2 lb (300 g) mozzarella
cheese

1 large bunch parsley

1 red bell pepper

2 cloves garlic

salt

freshly ground white pepper

1 quart (1 l) strong
vegetable stock (see page 29)

Preparation time:
About 40 minutes

34

Chickpea Soup with Spinach
From Greece • More time-consuming

• Let the chickpeas soak in a pan of water overnight.

• The next day, peel and chop the onions and garlic. Peel and dice the carrot, celery, and leek. Heat the oil in a large pot over medium heat. Add onions, garlic, carrot, celery, and leek, and braise until vegetables are translucent. Drain the chickpeas and add to pot.

• Stir in vegetable stock and bring to a boil. Cover the pot and cook over medium heat until chickpeas are done, about 1 hour.

• Meanwhile, pick over spinach, removing the thick stems, then wash in several changes of water. Wash the parsley and chop the leaves fine.

• When chickpeas are tender, add spinach to the pot and let it wilt in the soup for about 2 minutes. Season to taste with salt, white pepper, and lemon juice. Sprinkle with parsley, then serve. Makes 4 servings.

PER SERVING:	408 CALORIES	
NUTRITIONAL INFORMATION		
Carbohydrate	52	g
Protein	15	g
Total fat	18	g
Cholesterol	0	mg
Sodium	163	mg
Fiber	15	g

Bread Soup with Mozzarella
From Sardinia • Pictured

• Preheat oven to 400°F (200°C). Cut the bread into thin slices. Cut cheese into thin slices. Wash the parsley and chop it fine; set aside in a bowl. Remove the stem and the seeds from the pepper, and wash it under cold water; chop fine and add to bowl. Peel the garlic and chop it fine; add to bowl and toss to mix well.

• Fill a large ovenproof tureen with layers of bread and cheese, sprinkling some parsley mixture between the layers. Season with salt and pepper.

• Heat the vegetable stock, then pour over ingredients in the tureen. Put the tureen in the oven, and bake for about 20 minutes, or until the top is golden brown. Makes 4 servings.

PER SERVING:	297 CALORIES	
NUTRITIONAL INFORMATION		
Carbohydrate	30	g
Protein	19	g
Total fat	11	g
Cholesterol	33	mg
Sodium	610	mg
Fiber	4	g

Red Lentil Soup
From Turkey • Pictured

• Peel the onion and carrots and chop fine.

• Heat 1 tablespoon butter in a soup pot. Add onion and carrots and braise, stirring occasionally. Add lentils and cook briefly.

• Pour in the stock and bring to a boil. Season the soup with salt and pepper and cook, covered, over medium heat for about 20 minutes, or until the lentils are soft.

• Purée the soup in the pot with a hand blender or carefully transfer soup to a food processor and process to purée (this will have to be done in batches). Stir in lemon juice and yogurt. Taste and adjust seasonings.

• Cut the bread into cubes. In a large pan over medium-high heat, fry bread cubes in 1 tablespoon butter until golden brown. Melt remaining 2 tablespoons butter in a small pan with the paprika. Divide soup among 6 bowls.

• Garnish each with bread cubes and paprika butter, then serve. Makes 6 servings.

PER SERVING:	263 CALORIES	
NUTRITIONAL INFORMATION		
Carbohydrate	33	g
Protein	14	g
Total fat	9	g
Cholesterol	22	mg
Sodium	136	mg
Fiber	13	g

Cream of Pumpkin Soup
From France • Spicy

• Peel the pumpkin, remove the seeds and strings, and cut the flesh into small pieces. Trim the leek, wash it thoroughly, and slice into fine rings, including the green tops. Peel the potatoes and dice them fine.

• Heat the oil in a pot over medium heat. Add pumpkin, leek, and potatoes, and heat, stirring frequently, but do not brown.

• Pour in stock and bring to a boil. Let the soup boil, covered, over medium heat, for about 15 minutes, or until the potatoes are soft.

• Purée the soup in the pot with a hand blender or transfer to a food processor to purée. Season with salt, white pepper, cayenne, and lemon juice for a piquant taste. Serve the soup in warm soup bowls, garnished with a dollop of crème fraîche or sour cream. Makes 6 servings.

PER SERVING:	155 CALORIES	
NUTRITIONAL INFORMATION		
Carbohydrate	19	g
Protein	3	g
Total fat	9	g
Cholesterol	9	mg
Sodium	66	mg
Fiber	1	g

Red Lentil Soup

1 large onion

2 carrots

4 tablespoons (60 g) unsalted butter, divided

1/2 lb (200 g) red lentils

4³/4 cups (1¹/8 l) vegetable stock (see page 29)

salt

freshly ground white pepper

1 tablespoon fresh lemon juice

1 (8-oz/200-g) container plain yogurt

2 slices toasted bread

2 to 3 teaspoons Hungarian paprika or cayenne pepper

Preparation time:
About 40 minutes

Cream of Pumpkin Soup

1¹/2 lb (750 g) pumpkin

1 leek

2 (100–150 g) cooking potatoes

2 tablespoons olive oil

1 quart (1 l) vegetable stock (see page 29)

salt

freshly ground white pepper

cayenne pepper

1 tablespoon fresh lemon juice

1/2 cup (100 g) crème fraîche or sour cream

Preparation time:
About 40 minutes

10 small artichokes

5 to 6 tablespoons fresh
lemon juice, divided

3/4 lb (350 g) boiling potatoes

2 fennel bulbs

1 bunch scallions

3 tablespoons olive oil

1 teaspoon fennel greens

salt

freshly ground black pepper

1 package (300 g) thawed
frozen fava beans

1 cup (1/4 l) dry white wine

2 egg yolks

1/4 cup (60 ml) heavy cream

Preparation time:
About 1 1/4 hours

Vegetable Stew with Artichokes

From Greece • Classic

• Remove the hard outer leaves of the artichokes. Cut the other leaves in half. Quarter the artichokes lengthwise. Remove the choke. Mix the artichokes in a bowl with 3 to 4 tablespoons lemon juice.

• Peel the potatoes and cut into 3/4-inch- (2-cm) cubes. Wash fennel bulbs, trim, and cut lengthwise into small pieces. Reserve the delicate green part. Wash and trim scallions, then cut them into 1/2-inch-long (1-cm) pieces.

• Heat the oil in a large pot over medium heat. Add artichokes and sauté for about 5 minutes. Add potatoes, scallions, and fennel greens, and sear briefly. Add about 1 1/4 cups (300 ml) water. Season with salt and pepper and cook, covered, for about 10 minutes.

• Add fennel pieces, fava beans, and wine. Cook for 15 minutes more, or until artichokes and beans are soft.

• Meanwhile, chop fennel greens. In a small bowl, whisk together remaining lemon juice, egg yolks, and cream.

• Season the stew with salt and pepper, then remove from the stove; whisk in egg-yolk mixture. Sprinkle with fennel greens and serve. Makes 4 servings.

Variation from Turkey:
Vegetable Stew with Yogurt

Dice 2 zucchini and 1 eggplant. Quarter 4 green bell peppers. Dice 2 medium-size (250 g) peeled tomatoes. In a large pot, sear zucchini in 3 tablespoons oil. Add eggplant and 2 to 3 tablespoons more oil. Mix in 1 onion, chopped, and bell pepper pieces. Add tomatoes, 1 tablespoon tomato paste, and 1/2 cup (100 ml) water. Season with salt and pepper, then cook until vegetables are crisp-tender. In a small bowl, combine 1 3/4 cups (400 g) plain yogurt with 2 or 3 garlic cloves, pressed, then season to taste with salt, pepper, and lemon juice. Stir half of the yogurt mixture into the stew; serve the rest on the side.

PER SERVING:	550 CALORIES
NUTRITIONAL INFORMATION*	
Carbohydrate . . . . .75 g	
Protein . . . . .20 g	
Total fat . . . . .19 g	
Cholesterol . . . . .127 mg	
Sodium .384 mg	
Fiber . . . . .7 g	

*Refers to original recipe only.

WHAT
Would We Do Without ...

Pasta, Potatoes, and Rice

Simple, basic foods combined with subtle ingredients are the essence of Mediterranean cuisine. Whether you make the pasta yourself or buy it ready-made with spicy sauces, cook a luscious risotto, bake a pizza, or simply serve boiled potatoes with a zesty sauce, the most important aspect of the dishes in this chapter is the quality of the ingredients.

Pick Your Potato

Potato varieties differ primarily in their cooking characteristics. There are varieties of potatoes that cook firm, somewhat firm, and mealy. Always try to use the type of potato specified in each recipe. Gnocchi, for example, only succeeds with the mealy cooking variety, which are especially starchy. Firm-cooking potatoes are suitable for boiling, baking, and for salads. To ensure that the dishes become a real pleasure, you should get advice from the produce manager at your grocery store. Potatoes should be stored in a cool, dark area; otherwise they develop shoots and green spots. You must always cut out such parts, for they contain the toxin solanine.

The Right Rice

Rice for risotto, such as Arborio, is a short-grain rice. The grains are not washed before cooking because the finished risotto should be nicely moist and, therefore, the starch is important. For this reason, the dish is continually stirred during cooking, and the liquid is added little by little. You can buy Arborio rice in specialty groceries, and health-food stores. When using this variety, increase the cooking time by about 20 minutes, and increase the quantity of the liquid as well. Long-grain rice, cooked fluffy, is a suitable accompaniment to many dishes.

Fine Pasta-bilities

Pasta is available in supermarkets everywhere. Many kinds of Italian pasta taste especially good, for they are made with durum wheat and without eggs. This also applies to whole-wheat pasta. Try various kinds until you find your favorite brand. When cooking pasta, make sure that it doesn't get too soft. Follow the directions on the package. However, shortly before the cooking time is up, remove one strand from the pot to test for doneness.

Always use enough water to cook the pasta: about 1 quart (1 l) per ¼ pound (100 g) of pasta. Don't rinse the cooked pasta with cold water, but mix it with the sauce immediately after draining it; that way it won't stick together, and will stay nice and hot.

Cheese—The Ideal Partner

Freshly grated Parmesan cheese tastes delicious on pasta as well as on rice.

• Italy's Parmigiano-Reggiano is produced from April to November, and must age for at least eighteen months. The older it is, the sharper the taste becomes.

• The somewhat younger Grana Padano is produced throughout the year and must only be aged for twelve months. It is softer and melts faster on the hot pasta.

• Store a wedge of Parmesan in the refrigerator in the wrapper in which it was bought, or in plastic wrap (cut a few holes in it so the cheese doesn't sweat) for several weeks. Instead of Parmesan, aged Pecorino (available in good cheese stores) tastes good on pasta as well as on risotto. It has a somewhat sharper taste than Parmesan.

By the way: Don't buy Parmesan already grated; freshly grated tastes much better. There are numerous cheese graters on the market that can do this for you.

Pasta Makers—Not Only for Professionals

Anyone who likes to make pasta and ravioli, and makes it often, should get a pasta machine. Models with a hand crank are reasonably priced and do a good job. The machines have a smooth roller for flattening dough, which can be rolled to various thicknesses, according to how wide the roller space is set. These machines also have an attachment with which you can make spaghetti or tagliatelle.

Tagliatelle with Pesto
From Italy • Classic

• To make the pasta dough, mix the flour and the semolina with a large pinch of salt on a clean, dry surface. Make a well in the center and add the eggs and oil and gradually mix all ingredients. Knead to a smooth, supple dough. If it is too firm, add lukewarm water, one drop at a time. If you are using whole-wheat flour, refer to the note on page 5.

• Form the dough into a ball, wrap it in wax paper, and let it rest at room temperature for about 1 hour.

• Knead the dough once more and divide it into 4 portions. Working with one portion of dough, wrap remaining portions in a damp dish towel. Set the pasta machine on the widest setting to form a smooth slab of dough. Run the first portion of dough through the machine, then adjust the width to the next lowest setting. Continue to roll the dough through the machine, adjusting the setting smaller after each pass, until the dough is very thin. Place the dough through the tagliatelle roller to cut it into strips.

Repeat the process with the remaining dough. If you don't have a pasta machine, the dough must be rolled out as thin as possible, using as little flour as possible, then cut into broad noodles with a long knife.

• Spread the finished noodles on a floured dish towel and allow to dry for at least 1 hour, turning them once during the drying time.

• To make the pesto, wash the basil and arugula; shake them dry, and chop coarsely. Peel and mince the garlic.

• Mash the herbs, garlic, pine nuts, and walnuts to a fine paste in a mortar, or purée in a food processor. Mix in the cheese and oil, then season to taste with salt and pepper.

• Bring a large pot of salted water to a boil. Add the pasta and cook for about 3 minutes, or until *al dente*.

• In a warm dish, stir the pesto smooth by adding 1 to 2 tablespoons of the hot pasta water. Drain the tagliatelle, mix with the pesto in the dish, and serve immediately. Makes 6 servings.

PER SERVING:	703 CALORIES
NUTRITIONAL INFORMATION	
Carbohydrate 75	g
Protein 26	g
Total fat 36	g
Cholesterol 147	mg
Sodium 268	mg
Fiber 8	g

Tagliatelle with Pesto

For the pasta:
2 cups (200 g) white or whole-wheat flour (or spelt, see page 5)
2 cups (200 g) durum semolina flour
salt
4 eggs
1 tablespoon olive oil

For the pesto:
2 bunches basil
1 bunch arugula
2 cloves garlic
$^1/_2$ cup (50 g) pine nuts
$^1/_2$ cup (50 g) walnuts
$^1/_2$ cup (50 g) freshly grated Pecorino cheese
6 to 7 tablespoons (100 ml) olive oil
freshly ground white pepper

Preparation time:
About $1^1/_4$ hours (plus about 2 hours for resting)

45

Spaghetti with Arugula

2 cloves garlic

2 bunches (200 g) arugula

1 red bell pepper

1 lb (400 g) spaghetti

salt

$1/_4$ cup (60 ml) olive oil

freshly ground white pepper

$2/_3$ cup (150 g) ricotta cheese

*Preparation time:
About 25 minutes*

Vermicelli with Vegetables

1 eggplant

$1^1/_2$ lb (600 g) tomatoes

1 yellow bell pepper

2 cloves garlic

10 pitted black olives

1 bunch basil

$1/_4$ cup (60 ml) olive oil

2 to 3 teaspoons capers

1 small dried chili pepper,
optional

salt

freshly ground white pepper

1 lb (400 g) vermicelli

*Preparation time:
About 40 minutes*

Spaghetti with Arugula
From Italy • Spicy

• Peel the garlic and chop it fine. Wash the arugula, pat it dry, and chop fine. Remove the stem and seeds from the pepper and rinse under cold water, then cut into fine strips.

• Cook the spaghetti in a large pot of boiling salted water for about 8 minutes, or until *al dente.*

• Meanwhile, heat the oil in a pot over medium heat. Add garlic and pepper strips and sauté until tender. Add arugula and cook, stirring, for 5 minutes. Season to taste with salt and pepper, then spread the ricotta over top and keep warm, covered, off the heat.

• Drain the spaghetti and mix with the arugula sauce. Serve hot. Makes 4 servings.

PER SERVING:	608 CALORIES	
NUTRITIONAL INFORMATION		
Carbohydrate	89	g
Protein	20	g
Total fat	19	g
Cholesterol	13	mg
Sodium	62	mg
Fiber	3	g

Vermicelli with Vegetables
From Sicily • Pictured

• Wash the eggplant and cut into small cubes. Briefly immerse tomatoes in boiling water, then run under cold water and peel. Cut tomatoes into small cubes. Wash and seed the bell pepper, then cut into strips. Peel the garlic and chop fine. Cut olives in half. Wash basil and pull off the leaves.

• Heat oil in a large pot over medium heat. Add eggplant and brown well on all sides. Add bell pepper and garlic and cook briefly. Stir in tomatoes, olives, basil, capers, chili pepper, salt and white pepper. Cook for about 10 minutes, covered, over medium heat.

• Meanwhile, cook the vermicelli in a large pot of vigorously boiling salted water, for about 8 minutes, or until *al dente.*

• Drain the pasta, then mix with the sauce and serve immediately. Makes 4 servings.

PER SERVING:	657 CALORIES	
NUTRITIONAL INFORMATION		
Carbohydrate	105	g
Protein	12	g
Total fat	17	g
Cholesterol	0	mg
Sodium	400	mg
Fiber	10	g

Lasagna with Spinach and Ricotta
From Italy • A classic with a new treatment

• Pick over the spinach, removing the thick stems, and wash thoroughly in several changes of cold water. Bring a large pot of salted water to a boil. Add the spinach and blanch about 2 minutes. Drain spinach, running it under cold water. Allow spinach to drain completely before chopping coarsely.

• Peel the garlic and onion, then chop both fine. Heat 1 tablespoon oil in a large pan over medium heat. Add garlic and onion and sauté until tender. Add spinach and continue to cook, stirring, until the liquid has evaporated. Season with salt and pepper, then set aside.

• Peel and trim the carrot, celery, and leek, then chop fine. Heat remaining oil in a large pot. Add chopped vegetables and sear. Stir in the tomatoes. Add salt, white pepper, and crumbled chili pepper, if desired. Cook, uncovered, over medium heat for about 20 minutes, then set aside.

• Wash the herbs, remove the leaves and chop fine; stir herbs into the tomato sauce.

• Place ricotta in a sieve and press out liquid with a fork. Place drained ricotta, eggs, and half the Parmesan in a bowl; mix well. Add salt and white pepper, then set aside.

• Cook the lasagna in a large pot of boiling salted water for about 8 minutes, or until *al dente*. Rinse under cold water, then spread the strips out on the work surface. Cut the mozzarella in slices.

• Preheat the oven to 400°F (200°C). Fill a large baking dish in layers, starting with pasta, then some ricotta mixture, spinach, mozzarella slices, another layer of pasta, tomato sauce, spinach, and mozzarella, ending with another layer of pasta. Sprinkle remaining Parmesan on top and dot with butter.

• Bake lasagna for about 40 minutes, or until the top is golden brown. Makes 6 servings.

Lasagna with Spinach and Ricotta

2 lb (1 kg) spinach leaves

salt

2 cloves garlic

1 onion

2 tablespoons olive oil, divided

freshly ground white pepper

1 small carrot

1 stalk celery

1 leek

1 (28-oz/800-g) can peeled tomatoes, chopped

1 dried chili pepper, optional

4 to 5 sprigs rosemary

1 bunch basil

1 (15-oz/400-g) container ricotta cheese

2 eggs

1 cup (150 g) freshly grated Parmesan cheese

$^1/_2$ lb (250 g) lasagna noodles

$^1/_2$ lb (250 g) mozzarella cheese

1 tablespoon unsalted butter

Preparation time:
About 2$^1/_4$ hours (including 40 minutes for baking)

June 2020 - 4.5/5 very yummy but time consuming. Not sure I would bother boiling spinach.

PER SERVING:	476 CALORIES	
NUTRITIONAL INFORMATION		
Carbohydrate	31	g
Protein	32	g
Total fat	26	g
Cholesterol	149	mg
Sodium	827	mg
Fiber	5	g

For the dough:

4 cups (400 g) white or whole-wheat flour (or spelt, see page 5)

4 eggs

1 tablespoon olive oil

salt

For the filling:

1/2 lb (200 g) mascarpone cheese

1 egg

1/2 cup (50 g) freshly grated Parmesan cheese

2 teaspoons pesto (see page 45 or use ready-made)

salt

freshly ground white pepper

For the ragout:

3/4 lb (300 g) tomatoes

1 1/8 lb (500 g) pumpkin

1 large onion

2 cloves garlic

2 bunches basil

1 tablespoon olive oil

1/2 cup (100 ml) dry white wine or vegetable stock (see page 29)

pinch saffron threads

salt

freshly ground white pepper

freshly grated Parmesan cheese, optional

Preparation time: About 2 hours

Ravioli with Pumpkin Ragout

From Italy • More time-consuming

• In a large bowl, mix flour, eggs, and olive oil with 1 scant teaspoon salt; knead thoroughly until the dough is smooth and shiny. If you are using whole-wheat flour, refer to the note on page 5. Form the dough into a ball and let it rest, wrapped in plastic wrap, at room temperature while the filling and the pumpkin ragout are being prepared.

• In another bowl, mix the mascarpone, egg, Parmesan, and pesto; season to taste with salt and pepper. Set aside until ready to use.

• Briefly scald the tomatoes in a large pot of boiling water. Remove tomatoes from water and skin them, then cut into small cubes. Peel and seed the pumpkin, then dice the flesh. Peel the onion and garlic and mince fine. Wash the basil and shake it dry; remove and discard stems.

• Heat the oil in a large pot over medium heat. Add onion and garlic and sauté 1 minute. Add the pumpkin and cook several minutes. Stir in tomatoes, wine, and basil. Mix in the saffron. Season with salt and pepper, then cook, covered, over medium heat, for about 10 minutes. Set aside, keeping warm, until ready to use.

• Meanwhile, knead the pasta dough thoroughly once more. Divide the dough in half and roll it out on a floured surface to a little more than 1/16 inch (2 mm) thick.

• Using one half of the dough, place 1 teaspoon of the mascarpone filling on the dough at intervals of about 1 inch (3 cm); cover with the other piece of dough.

• Gently press the dough together around the mounds of filling. Using a pastry wheel, cut between the mounds to make raviolis. Press the edges of the dough together with a fork.

• Bring a large pot of salted water to a boil. Add ravioli and cook for about 3 minutes. Drain ravioli and mix with the sauce before serving on warm plates. Top each serving with grated Parmesan. Makes 6 servings.

PER SERVING:	522 CALORIES
NUTRITIONAL INFORMATION	

Carbohydrate	77	g
Protein	24	g
Total fat	11	g
Cholesterol	185	mg
Sodium	498	mg
Fiber	4	g

Swiss Chard Risotto

From Italy • Pictured

• Wash the Swiss chard and trim. Cut the leaves into strips and chop the stems fine. Peel and dice the carrot, celery, and leek. Wash and zest the lemon. Peel and chop garlic.

• In a large saucepan, heat half the butter. Add the carrot, celery, leek, and garlic and braise until vegetables are tender. Add rice and continue cooking, stirring. Add the Swiss chard and briefly braise with the other vegetables.

• In a small saucepan, heat the wine and stock. Stir 1 cup of the stock mixture into the rice. Add tomato paste, lemon zest, and capers, and continue to cook, stirring, until the liquid is absorbed.

• Add another cup of stock and let the mixture cook down. Stir in the remaining stock, and cook, covered, over medium heat for another 20 minutes, stirring occasionally; if necessary, add about 1/2 cup (100 ml) water.

• Mix in the remaining butter and the Parmesan and season with salt and pepper. Makes 4 servings.

PER SERVING:	627 CALORIES	
NUTRITIONAL INFORMATION		
Carbohydrate	103	g
Protein	14	g
Total fat	13	g
Cholesterol	32	mg
Sodium	492	mg
Fiber	5	g

Artichoke Risotto

From Italy • Classic

• Quarter the artichoke hearts. Peel the lemon and dice the fruit. Wash and finely chop the arugula. Trim the scallions and slice them thin.

• Heat half the butter. Add scallions and braise until they are translucent. Add rice and continue cooking, but do not brown. Add arugula and briefly braise with the rice mixture.

• Add about 1 cup stock, artichoke quarters, and lemon pieces to the rice. Let simmer, uncovered, until the liquid has been absorbed, stirring occasionally.

• Add another cup of stock and let it reduce. Stir in remaining stock, and cook, covered, over medium heat for about 20 more minutes, stirring occasionally; if necessary, add about 1/2 cup (100 ml) water.

• Dice the Gorgonzola and mix it into the risotto with the remaining butter; season with salt and pepper. Makes 4 servings.

Oct 2014 3/5
was ok but had a bitter
taste. There are better
recipes out there

PER SERVING:	567 CALORIES	
NUTRITIONAL INFORMATION		
Carbohydrate	97	g
Protein	12	g
Total fat	14	g
Cholesterol	35	mg
Sodium	310	mg
Fiber	4	g

Swiss Chard Risotto

1/2 lb (200 g) Swiss chard

1 small carrot

1 stalk celery

1 leek

1/2 lemon

1 or 2 cloves garlic

3 tablespoons unsalted butter, divided

1 lb (400 g) Arborio rice

1 cup (1/4 l) dry white wine

3 cups (3/4 l) vegetable stock (see page 29)

2 teaspoons tomato paste

1 teaspoon capers

1/2 cup (50 g) freshly grated Parmesan cheese

salt

freshly ground white pepper

Preparation time:
About 1 hour

Artichoke Risotto

8 canned artichoke hearts, rinsed and drained

1 lemon

1 bunch (50 g) arugula

2 scallions

3 tablespoons unsalted butter, divided

1 lb (400 g) Arborio rice

1 quart (1 l) vegetable stock

2 oz (50 g) Gorgonzola cheese

salt

freshly ground white pepper

Preparation time:
About 45 minutes

Tomato Mozzarella Pizza

Tomato Mozzarella Pizza

For the dough:

2¹/₂ cups (300 g) white or whole-wheat flour (or spelt, see page 5)

salt

4 tablespoons olive oil

1 package (20 g) active dry yeast

For the topping:

2¹/₄ lb (1 kg) ripe tomatoes

2 onions

3 cloves garlic

salt

freshly ground white pepper

³/₄ lb (375 g) mozzarella cheese

1 bunch basil

1 tablespoon capers

4 whole hot red peppers (from a jar)

Preparation time: About 1³/₄ hours

Tomato Mozzarella Pizza
From Italy • Spicy

• Mix the flour, a large pinch of salt, and 4 tablespoons oil in a bowl. In a small bowl, empty the yeast into about ¹/₂ cup (100 ml) lukewarm water; stir to dissolve. Add yeast mixture to flour and knead to a smooth, elastic dough. Allow dough to rise, covered, for 45 minutes, or until doubled in bulk. If you are using whole-wheat flour, refer to the note on page 5.

• In the meantime, peel and dice tomatoes. Peel the onion and garlic and chop them fine.

• Heat 1 tablespoon oil in a large pot. Add onions and garlic and sauté until they are translucent. Add tomatoes, and allow the sauce to cook, uncovered, over medium heat for about 30 minutes, or until sauce is very thick. Season with salt and pepper.

• Cut the mozzarella into thin slices. Wash the basil, pull off the leaves, and pat them dry. Brush a baking sheet with oil and preheat the oven to 425°F (220°C).

• Knead the dough again, then roll it out on a floured surface to the size of the baking sheet. Lay the dough on the oiled sheet, making the edges somewhat thicker. Spread the tomato sauce on the dough, and top with basil, capers, peppers, and mozzarella; drizzle 1 tablespoon olive oil over top.

• Bake the pizza until brown, about 20 minutes. Makes 4 servings.

Variation from France: Pissaladière

In a large pan over medium heat, fry 1³/₄ lb (800 g) chopped onions in 2 tablespoons oil for about 15 minutes. When they are translucent, cover the rolled-out dough on the baking sheet with a mixture of onions, 2 pressed garlic cloves, salt, pepper, and 3 teaspoons tomato paste. Top with 2 fresh tomatoes, sliced, and 20 black olives; sprinkle with 1 cup (100 g) grated Gruyère, and bake.

April 2018 - yummy but crust was not light and fluffy, probably our climate. Had to use almost double the water. Sauce was too acidy for Kyky

54

PER SERVING:	672 CALORIES
NUTRITIONAL INFORMATION*	
Carbohydrate . . . . 73 g	
Protein . . . . 31 g	
Total fat . . . . 28 g	
Cholesterol . . . . 49 mg	
Sodium . . . . 629 mg	
Fiber . . . . 5 g	

Refers to original recipe only.

Potatoes with Nut Sauce

From Spain • Pictured

• Preheat the oven to 475°F (250°C). Wash the pepper, cut it in half, and remove the seeds. Place pepper halves in the oven for about 20 minutes, or until the skin is blistered and brown.

• Let the pepper rest under a damp towel, and then pull off and discard the skin. Coarsely chop the pepper and place in a food processor. Briefly immerse the tomatoes in boiling water. Remove the skins, and dice; add to chopped peppers. Crumble dried peppers into processor. Peel and quarter garlic cloves; add to processor. Roast the nuts in a dry pan over medium heat until they smell fragrant, then add to processor. Process to purée. While processing, add the oil in a thin stream. Season the sauce to taste with lemon juice and salt, then set aside.

• Wash potatoes. Place them in a large pot with enough water to cover. Bring to a boil and cook potatoes until soft, about 20 minutes. Drain and with a knife make a slit in center of each potato and pinch open. Top with sauce. Makes 4 servings.

PER SERVING:	357 CALORIES
NUTRITIONAL INFORMATION	
Carbohydrate . . . . 36 g	
Protein . . . . 7 g	
Total fat . . . . 23 g	
Cholesterol . . . . 0 mg	
Sodium . . . . 110 mg	
Fiber . . . . 6 g	

Potato Omelet

From Spain • Easy to make

• Wash and peel the potatoes. Cut them into 1/8-inch- (3-cm) thick slices, and pat them dry with a towel.

• In a large bowl, beat the eggs until they are foamy. Add salt and pepper.

• Heat the oil in a large pan over medium heat. Add potatoes and sauté, turning constantly, for about 3 minutes, or until they are golden brown.

• Pour eggs over the potatoes, and cook the omelet, covered, over low heat for about 8 minutes, or until it is brown and can be lifted out of the pan.

• Slide the omelet onto a plate. Invert a second plate over the omelet, then turn it over and return the omelet to the pan. Cook, covered, for about 5 minutes more, or until done. The omelet should be browned and the potatoes soft. Serve with a tossed salad. Makes 4 servings.

PER SERVING:	310 CALORIES
NUTRITIONAL INFORMATION	
Carbohydrate . . . . 23 g	
Protein . . . . 10 g	
Total fat . . . . 20 g	
Cholesterol . . . . 265 mg	
Sodium . . . . 157 mg	
Fiber . . . . 2 g	

57

For the gnocchi:

2$^1/_8$ lb (1 kg) cooking
potatoes

2 cups (200 g) white or
whole-wheat flour (or spelt,
see page 5)

salt

1 egg yolk

$^1/_2$ cup (50 g) freshly grated
Parmesan cheese

For the herb butter:

1 large bunch basil

1 large bunch borage or
$^1/_2$ cup (50 g) small spinach
leaves

2 cloves garlic

salt

5 tablespoons (75 g)
unsalted butter

pinch saffron threads

freshly ground white pepper

freshly grated Parmesan
cheese, optional

Preparation time:
About 2 hours

Gnocchi with Herb-Saffron Butter

From Italy • More time-consuming

• To make the gnocchi, wash the potatoes and cook them in a large pot of water, covered, over medium heat for about 30 minutes, or until they are soft.

• Peel the potatoes while still hot, and immediately put them through a food mill, then into a bowl.

• Allow the purée to cool somewhat, then stir in the flour, salt, egg yolk, and cheese; knead briefly but thoroughly.

• On a lightly floured working area, form rolls of the dough about as thick as your index finger. Cut the rolls into $^3/_4$-inch- (2-cm) long pieces, then press each a little with a fork.

• Lay the gnocchi on a floured dish towel and let rest for about 15 minutes.

• Wash basil and borage, shake dry, and remove any large, coarse stems. Chop the leaves coarsely. Peel and mince the garlic. Set greens and garlic aside.

• Bring a large pot of salted water to a boil. Add half of the gnocchi. As soon as the gnocchi rise to the surface, lift them out with a slotted spoon or skimmer. Place gnocchi in a dish, and keep them warm in a 150°F (75°C) oven while cooking the remaining gnocchi.

• In the meantime, melt the butter in a large pan over medium heat. Add the greens, garlic, and saffron, and let them wilt while stirring. Season with salt and pepper.

• Gently toss gnocchi with the herb butter, then divide among 4 plates. Serve with freshly grated Parmesan on top. Makes 4 servings.

PER SERVING:	626 CALORIES
NUTRITIONAL INFORMATION	
Carbohydrate . . . . .95 g	
Protein . . . . .16 g	
Total fat . . . . .20 g	
Cholesterol . . . . .102 mg	
Sodium . . . . .352 mg	
Fiber . . . . .6 g	

A PASSION FOR
FOR

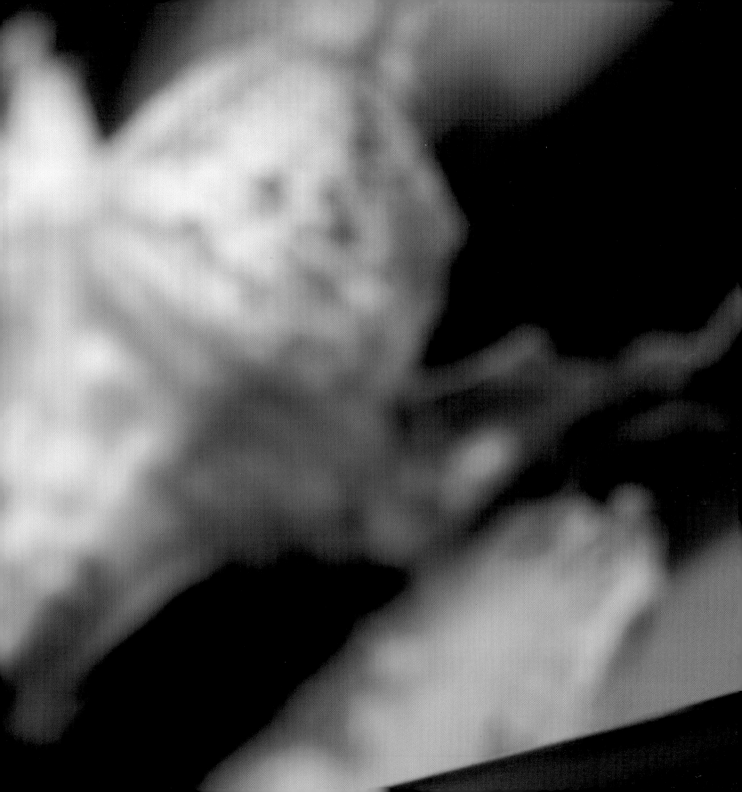

Vegetables

The fertile soil and blazing sunshine in the Mediterranean regions guarantee ideal conditions for a rich selection of vegetables. No wonder, then, that vegetables are central in this cuisine, not only for appetizers and soups, but also for main dishes. You are, most likely, very familiar with the vegetables below, but we've added some helpful hints to their descriptions.

Summer Variety

• Eggplant is surely familiar. However, the symmetrical, almost uniformly shaped vegetables from the supermarket often are a disappointment when it comes to taste. If eggplants are harvested too early, not only do they lack flavor, but they also can contain the toxin solanine. Thus, you should always cut out the green spots in eggplants! When eggplants are ripe, the skin is no longer very shiny, and the flesh gives a little with pressure. You should use eggplants as soon as possible after buying them; they don't store very well.

• Squash, a close relative of zucchini, is sold in various kinds and sizes. Larger squashes can be purchased in whatever size you want in the market. In case there is some left over, you can keep the squash in the refrigerator, covered with plastic wrap, for about three days. Whole squash, on the other hand, can be stored in a cool place for several weeks.

• Swiss chard also grows wild in the Mediterranean countries and is not related to spinach, but to the red beet. Nevertheless, this flavorful vegetable, which unfortunately is relatively rare here, is best replaced by the sturdy curly spinach.

• Okra, used primarily in Greece and Turkey, often accompanies meat, and is stewed with tomatoes as well. The ridged pods of okra can grow up to 6 inches (15 cm) long, and are harvested unripe. During cooking, sliced okra will secrete a somewhat milky viscous fluid, which serves as a thickening agent. If desired, blanch the pods for about 3 minutes in boiling water with a shot of vinegar before using in a recipe. Okra pods should be firm and green when you buy them, and no more than 3 inches long, to enjoy them at their most tender.

• Spinach has sturdy, thick, curly leaves, in which dirt and sand usually collect. Spinach should be thoroughly washed in at least two changes of cold water. A finer-leaf spinach has smaller, smooth leaves, which usually are not so dirty. Spinach can be eaten raw in salads, or can be cooked.

Sun-ripened Freshness

All vegetables are best when bought in season, particularly if they are harvested after being sun-ripened. To help you remember when produce is in season, we have created a calendar of vegetable seasons on the inside front cover. Furthermore, vegetables such as tomatoes and peppers should not be kept in the refrigerator, but should be stored at room temperature; otherwise, they will lose their flavor.

Additions for Nonvegetarians

To go along with the vegetable dishes, prepare your favorite fish, seasoned, then grilled or baked.

Deep-fat Frying—Crispy Jackets for Tender Vegetables

A popular method for preparing vegetables in the Mediterranean countries is deep-fat frying in batter.

For the batter, you need about 1 1/2 cups (175 g) flour, 2 eggs, about 1 scant cup (175 ml) water, 2 tablespoons olive oil, and a generous pinch of salt.

Stir all the ingredients together and let stand for 30 minutes. Slice, cube, or chop as necessary potatoes, mushrooms, zucchini, peppers, or onions; you also may use zucchini flowers. Coat vegetables in batter, then fry in hot oil. Tzatziki (see page 12) or Nut Sauce (see page 57) are good accompaniments, but a garlic mayonnaise also is very good.

Ratatouille
From France • Pictured

• Peel the onion and slice into thin rings. Peel the eggplants and cut into 3/4-inch- (2-cm) cubes. Wash and dice the zucchini. Briefly immerse the tomatoes in boiling water; remove from water, peel, and slice. Wash the peppers, remove the seeds, and cut into pieces. Peel the garlic and slice very thin.

• In a large pot, heat 3 tablespoons oil. Add eggplant and sauté, stirring vigorously. Add the remaining 2 tablespoons oil, onion, zucchini, garlic, and peppers. Sauté vegetables for a few minutes, stirring to keep them from browning. Add the tomatoes and about 1/2 cup (100 ml) water; add salt and pepper. Wash the herbs, removing stems, and add the leaves to the mixture.

• Simmer over low heat for about 30 minutes. Remove the herbs, taste the ratatouille and adjust seasonings, then serve hot, room temperature, or cold. Makes 4 servings.

PER SERVING:	289 CALORIES	
NUTRITIONAL INFORMATION		
Carbohydrate	32	g
Protein	6	g
Total fat	18	g
Cholesterol	0	mg
Sodium	99	mg
Fiber	11	g

Sicilian Eggplant
From Italy • Spicy

• Wash the celery, remove strings, and cut into thin slices. Peel the onion and chop it fine. Wash the eggplants, trim, and cut them into small dice. Briefly immerse the tomatoes in boiling water; remove from water, peel, and dice.

• Heat 2 tablespoons oil in a large pot over medium heat. Add celery and onion and braise until translucent. Add eggplant and the remaining 2 tablespoons oil; continue to braise, stirring, until the eggplant is slightly browned. Mix in the tomatoes.

• Add olives to the vegetables. Stir in vinegar, sugar, salt, and pepper, then simmer the vegetables, covered, over low heat for about 10 minutes.

• Mix in capers and pine nuts, then season to taste once again. Serve warm with potatoes, pasta, or rice, or cold as an appetizer. Makes 4 servings.

Nov 24th - 3.5/5
Yummy. Didn't include pine nuts and didn't peel tomato

PER SERVING:	250 CALORIES	
NUTRITIONAL INFORMATION		
Carbohydrate	26	g
Protein	5	g
Total fat	17	g
Cholesterol	0	mg
Sodium	292	mg
Fiber	8	g

Ratatouille

1 white onion

2 eggplants

2 zucchini

1 1/8 lb (500 g) plum tomatoes

1 red bell pepper

1 green bell pepper

2 cloves garlic

5 tablespoons olive oil, divided

salt

freshly ground white pepper

sprigs of fresh thyme

1/2 bunch parsley

1 bay leaf

Preparation time: About 1 hour

Sicilian Eggplant

1/2 bunch celery

1 onion

2 eggplants

1 lb (400 g) tomatoes

4 tablespoons olive oil, divided

10 pitted black olives

2 tablespoons red wine vinegar

pinch sugar

salt

freshly ground white pepper

2 teaspoons capers

2 teaspoons pine nuts

Preparation time: About 45 minutes

For the onion-nut sauce:
1 lb (400 g) onions
1/2 cup (50 g) walnut pieces
1/2 cup (100 ml) olive oil
1 teaspoon dried herbes de Provence
salt
freshly ground white pepper
large pinch cinnamon

For the vegetables:
1 medium-size eggplant
2 large zucchini

For the tomato sauce:
1 lb (500 g) tomatoes
2 cloves garlic
1 bunch (50 g) parsley

For the cream sauce:
3 tablespoons (40 g) unsalted butter, divided
1/2 cup (40 g) white or whole-wheat flour (or spelt, see page 5)
2 cups (450 ml) milk
1/2 cup (125 g) freshly grated Parmesan cheese
freshly grated nutmeg
fresh lemon juice
2 eggs
1 lb (500 g) cooking potatoes

Preparation time:
About 2 1/2 hours (including 1 hour for baking)

66

Moussaka with Onion-Nut Sauce
From Greece • More time-consuming

• To make the onion-nut sauce, peel the onions and chop fine. Chop the walnut pieces very fine. Heat 2 tablespoons oil in a large pot over medium heat. Add onions and herbs and sauté, stirring, until soft, about 15 minutes. Add nuts and sauté briefly. Season with salt, pepper, and cinnamon to taste; set aside.

• To make the vegetables, wash the eggplant and zucchini; trim and slice thin lengthwise. Cut eggplant slices in half crosswise. Heat 1 tablespoon oil in a large pot over medium heat. Add eggplant and zucchini, a few slices at a time, and sauté to brown on both sides, and set them aside.

• To make the tomato sauce, briefly immerse tomatoes in boiling water; remove from water and peel, then dice them fine. Peel and mince the garlic fine. Wash the parsley and chop it fine.

• Heat about 1/3 cup (75 ml) oil in another large pot over medium heat. Add tomato, parsley, and garlic, and sauté without browning; let the vegetables cook down until soft, then add salt and pepper; set aside.

• To make the cream sauce, melt 2 tablespoons butter in a saucepan. Whisk in the flour. Heat milk in another saucepan, but do not boil.

Whisk hot milk into butter mixture, then simmer over low heat for about 5 minutes, stirring occasionally.

• Stir Parmesan into the milk mixture, then season to taste with salt, pepper, nutmeg, and lemon juice. Beat eggs in a small bowl. Add about 1/4 cup (60 ml) hot milk mixture into beaten eggs, then whisk egg mixture into milk mixture to finish cream sauce; set aside.

• Wash the potatoes, peel, and slice very thin. Preheat oven to 350°F (180°C).

• Fill a large baking dish with layers of potatoes, onion sauce, tomato sauce, zucchini, and eggplant, beginning with the potatoes and ending with the eggplant. Spoon some cream sauce over each layer. Pour the remaining cream sauce over top, and dot with remaining tablespoon of butter.

• Put the moussaka in the oven and bake for about 1 hour, or until the potatoes are soft and the surface is nicely browned. Makes 6 servings.

PER SERVING:	550 CALORIES	
NUTRITIONAL INFORMATION		
Carbohydrate	46	g
Protein	16	g
Total fat	36	g
Cholesterol	98	mg
Sodium	258	mg
Fiber	7	g

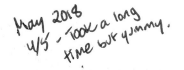
May 2018
4/5 - Took a long time but yummy.

Okra with Tomatoes
From Turkey • Pictured

• Wash the okra and cut off the stems.

• Peel the onion and garlic and chop fine. Briefly immerse tomatoes in boiling water; remove from water, peel, and cut into small cubes.

• Heat the oil in a large pot over medium heat. Add onion and garlic and sauté until translucent. Add okra and sauté briefly.

• Add the tomatoes and about $1/3$ cup (80 ml) water. Season with salt, pepper, and paprika, then stew, covered, over low heat for about 10 minutes.

• In the meantime, wash the parsley and chop it fine. Stir parsley and lemon juice into the vegetables during the last 5 minutes of cooking time.

• Season with salt and pepper to taste, then serve. Rice, millet, or boiled bulgur are good accompaniments. Makes 4 servings.

PER SERVING:	192 CALORIES	
NUTRITIONAL INFORMATION		
Carbohydrate	23	g
Protein	5	g
Total fat	11	g
Cholesterol	0	mg
Sodium	101	mg
Fiber	5	g

Stewed Eggplant
From Turkey • Perfect for company

• Wash the eggplants and peel lengthwise in strips about $1/2$ inch ($1^1/2$ cm) apart (peel one strip and leave one strip on); at one place, cut a gash about $3/4$ inch (2 cm) deep and $1/4$ inch ($1/2$ cm) wide along the length of each eggplant.

• Peel the onions and slice into rings. Peel and dice the tomatoes. Wash and seed the peppers; chop them fine. Wash the parsley and chop it fine. Peel and mince the garlic.

• Heat 3 tablespoons oil in a medium-size saucepan over medium heat. Add onions and sauté until they are translucent. Add tomatoes, peppers, and parsley, and sauté about 5 minutes. Season to taste with garlic, salt, pepper, and paprika.

• Heat remaining 3 tablespoons oil in a large pot over medium heat. Add eggplants and sear all over. Arrange them in the pot with the gashes on top. Spread the tomato mixture into the gashes. Pour in $1/2$ cup (100 ml) water, bring to a boil, and simmer over low heat, covered, for 20–30 minutes, or until soft. Makes 4 servings.

PER SERVING:	380 CALORIES	
NUTRITIONAL INFORMATION		
Carbohydrate	47	g
Protein	8	g
Total fat	22	g
Cholesterol	0	mg
Sodium	105	mg
Fiber	16	g

Okra with Tomatoes

$1^1/2$ lb (700 g) medium-size okra pods

1 large onion

2 or 3 cloves garlic

1 lb (400 g) tomatoes

3 tablespoons olive oil

salt

freshly ground white pepper

$1/2$ teaspoon Hungarian paprika

1 bunch parsley

1 tablespoon fresh lemon juice

*Preparation time:
About 40 minutes*

Stewed Eggplant

4 eggplants

2 onions

2 large tomatoes

2 green bell peppers

1 to 2 bunches parsley

4 cloves garlic

6 tablespoons olive oil, divided

salt

freshly ground white pepper

pinch Hungarian paprika

*Preparation time:
About 1 hour*

Stuffed Peppers and Tomatoes

From Italy • Spicy

• For the peppers, preheat the oven to 475°F (250°C). Wash and seed the peppers, and lay them on a baking sheet. Bake for about 25 minutes, or until the skins are blistered.

• Let the peppers cool briefly under a damp towel. Carefully pull off the skins, then cut the pepper flesh lengthwise into 4 pieces.

• While the peppers are baking, soften the roll in water. Place olives, capers, and pine nuts in the bowl of a food processor and process to chop fine. Wash the parsley and chop fine. Press the water out of the roll and tear it into pieces. In a large bowl, combine olive mixture, parsley, bread, egg, salt, and pepper, mixing well.

• Cover each pepper slice with some of the mixture, and roll them up lengthwise. Lay stuffed peppers, cut side down, in a buttered baking dish; set aside.

• Wash the tomatoes and cut a little lid in each one. Spoon out the pulp and chop it fine. Wash the basil and chop the leaves. Peel and mince the garlic.

• Heat oil in a saucepan over medium heat. Add tomato pulp and garlic, and cook, stirring occasionally, for about 10 minutes, or until soft.

• Remove tomato mixture from the stove and allow it to cool somewhat. Break ricotta into small clumps and stir into the tomato mixture, along with the basil and Pecorino. Season the mixture with salt, pepper, and lemon juice, then fill the tomatoes.

• Preheat the oven to 400°F (200°C). Lay the tomatoes in the dish next to the pepper rolls, and drizzle olive oil over the vegetables.

• Bake the vegetables for about 30 minutes, or until they are nicely browned. Makes 4 servings.

Nov 2019 - Did just the peppers. OK.. left peel on.

PER SERVING:	372 CALORIES
NUTRITIONAL INFORMATION	

Carbohydrate	35	g
Protein	14	g
Total fat	23	g
Cholesterol	64	mg
Sodium	690	mg
Fiber	8	g

Stuffed Peppers and Tomatoes

For the peppers:
4 yellow bell peppers
1 dinner roll
15 pitted green olives
$1/4$ cup (50 g) capers
$1/4$ cup (50 g) pine nuts
1 bunch parsley
1 egg
salt
freshly ground white pepper

For the tomatoes:
8 medium-size tomatoes
1 bunch basil
2 cloves garlic
1 tablespoon olive oil
$3^1/2$ oz (100 g) firm ricotta or other fresh cheese
2 tablespoons freshly grated Pecorino or Parmesan cheese
salt
freshly ground white pepper
1 teaspoon fresh lemon juice

For drizzling:
2 tablespoons olive oil

For the dish:
Unsalted butter

Preparation time:
About $1^3/4$ hours (including 55 minutes for baking)

Swiss Chard with Raisins

2 lb (1 kg) Swiss chard

salt

3 cloves garlic

1/4 cup (60 ml) olive oil

1/4 cup (50 g) pine nuts

1/4 cup (50 g) raisins

1 tablespoon fresh lemon juice

freshly ground white pepper

Preparation time:
About 30 minutes

Mixed Vegetable Gratin

1 1/2 lb (700 g) tomatoes

1 2/3 lb (750 g) pumpkin

1 2/3 lb (750 g) eggplant

salt

1 1/8 lb (500 g) mild white onions

8 tablespoons olive oil, divided

1 cup (250 g) freshly grated Pecorino cheese

freshly ground white pepper

1/4 cup (50 g) bread crumbs

Preparation time:
About 1 hour 20 minutes (including 30 minutes for baking)

Swiss Chard with Raisins
From Spain • Pictured

• Wash and trim the Swiss chard. Cut off the leaves and chop them coarsely. Cut the stems into crosswise strips.

• Bring a large pot of salted water to boil. Add stems and blanch for about 2 minutes. Add the leaves and blanch for about 1 minute more. Drain in a colander and run under cold water to stop the cooking.

• Peel and mince the garlic. Heat the oil in a large pan over medium heat. Add pine nuts and toast, stirring frequently. Add raisins and garlic, and sauté briefly.

• Add the Swiss chard, then season with lemon juice, salt, and pepper; simmer, covered, over low heat for about 5 more minutes.

• This dish can be served hot as a side dish, or room temperature or cold as an appetizer. Makes 4 servings.

PER SERVING:	245 CALORIES	
NUTRITIONAL INFORMATION		
Carbohydrate	18	g
Protein	7	g
Total fat	19	g
Cholesterol	0	mg
Sodium	558	mg
Fiber	5	g

Mixed Vegetable Gratin
From France • More time-consuming

• Briefly immerse the tomatoes in boiling water; remove from water and peel, then cut horizontally into thin slices. Peel the pumpkin and cut the flesh into 1/4-inch- (1/2-cm) thick slices. Wash the eggplant, trim, and slice about 1/2 inch (1 cm) thick.

• Bring a large pot of salted water to a boil. Add the pumpkin and eggplant and blanch for about 5 minutes; drain in a colander and run under cold water to stop the cooking.

• Peel the onions and slice into fine rings. Heat 2 tablespoons oil in a large pan over medium heat. Add onions and sauté until lightly brown.

• Preheat the oven to 350°F (180°C). Fill baking dish with alternating layers of onions, tomatoes, pumpkin, and eggplant. Season each layer with salt, pepper, and some cheese.

• Mix the remaining cheese with bread crumbs, then sprinkle on the vegetables. Drizzle the remaining oil over top.

• Bake for about 30 minutes, or until brown. Makes 4 servings.

PER SERVING:	509 CALORIES	
NUTRITIONAL INFORMATION		
Carbohydrate	42	g
Protein	14	g
Total fat	34	g
Cholesterol	16	mg
Sodium	524	mg
Fiber	4	g

Vegetable-Cheese Pie

1 (10¹/₂-oz/300-g) package frozen puff pastry or phyllo dough (see note)

¹/₄ cup (50 g) unsalted butter, melted

1²/₃ lb (750 g) spinach or a combination of spinach and escarole

salt

1 head (200 g) curly endive

1 bunch scallions

1 large onion

2 tablespoons olive oil

freshly ground white pepper

freshly grated nutmeg

1 tablespoon fennel seeds

1 large bunch dill

3 eggs

¹/₂ lb (250 g) feta cheese

1 egg yolk

2 tablespoons milk

Preparation time: About 1³/₄ hours (including 55 minutes for baking)

Vegetable-Cheese Pie
From Greece • Perfect for company

• Spread out the pastry sheets next to one another on wax paper. (See note below for phyllo dough.)

• Wash the spinach thoroughly in several changes of cold water, then blanch in boiling salted water for about 4 minutes. Drain spinach in a colander, then rinse under cold water; drain well. Press out excess water with your hands, then chop the spinach fine.

• Wash the endive and cut into fine strips. Wash and trim the scallions, then cut into fine slices, including the bright green tops. Peel the onion and chop fine.

• Heat oil in a large pan over medium heat. Add onion, scallions, and endive, and sauté a few minutes, stirring, until they are tender. Add the spinach, and cook only until they are no longer damp. Season to taste with salt, pepper, and nutmeg. Crack the fennel seeds on a wooden board with the flat side of a wide knife, then add them to the vegetables.

• Wash the dill and chop it fine. In a small bowl, lightly beat the whole eggs. Crumble the feta into the vegetables, then stir in dill and beaten eggs.

• Preheat the oven to 350°F (180°C). Rinse out an 11-inch springform pan with cold water. For puff pastry, lay 3 sheets of pastry on top of one another; using a little flour, roll out into a round slab, which should be a little larger than the pan. Lay the dough in the pan, allowing it to hang over the edge on the outside.

Note: If you are using phyllo dough, work very fast as it has a tendency to dry out. Lay 1 sheet on wax paper, brush with melted butter, then lay the next sheet on top of the first, brush with butter, then repeat process for third sheet. Stack the 3 sheets of dough in the pan.

• Distribute the filling on the dough. Fold the edges on top of the filling. Using another 3 sheets of dough, repeat the above process. Roll the dough into a round. Lay the dough over the filling. In a small bowl, mix the egg yolk with the milk. Brush the yolk mixture on the dough.

• Bake the pie for about 55 minutes, or until it is golden brown on top. Makes 4 servings.

PER SERVING:	681 CALORIES
NUTRITIONAL INFORMATION	

Carbohydrate	55	g
Protein	26	g
Total fat	41	g
Cholesterol	296	mg
Sodium	1282	mg
Fiber	8	g

76

Vegetable Gratin with Feta Cheese

From Greece • Pictured

• Wash the peppers, seed them, and cut them into strips. Wash and trim the zucchini and eggplant, then dice them. Wash the tomatoes and slice horizontally, across the seed chambers.

• Heat the oil in a large pot over medium heat. Add zucchini, eggplant, and peppers, and sauté, stirring for several minutes. Stir in the herbs and tomatoes.

• Peel the garlic; put it through a press into vegetable mixture. Sauté to heat through. Add salt and pepper, then pour vegetable mixture into a baking dish. Preheat the oven to 400°F (200°C).

• In a medium-size bowl, blend the cheese with the milk; beat in the eggs. Season with pepper and a little salt.

• Pour the egg-cheese mixture over the vegetables and top with olives and hot peppers. Bake about 45 minutes, or until gratin is nicely browned. Makes 4 servings.

Spinach with Yogurt

From Turkey • Exotic

• Pick over the spinach, and wash it thoroughly in several changes of cold water. Bring a large pot of salted water to boil. Add spinach.

• Let the spinach boil vigorously, covered, for about 3 minutes, or until all the leaves have wilted.

• Rinse the spinach in a colander under cold water, and allow it to drain thoroughly. Press out excess liquid with your hands, then chop spinach very fine. Peel the onion and garlic and chop them fine.

• Heat the oil in a large pot over medium heat. Add onion and garlic and sauté, stirring to keep it from browning, for about 3 minutes. Add spinach and braise several minutes more.

• Stir in yogurt, then season the spinach with cumin, salt, pepper, and lemon juice. Serve room temperature or cold as a side dish. Makes 4 servings.

PER SERVING:	545 CALORIES	
NUTRITIONAL INFORMATION		
Carbohydrate	32	g
Protein	22	g
Total fat	39	g
Cholesterol	237	mg
Sodium	1258	mg
Fiber	8	g

PER SERVING:	134 CALORIES	
NUTRITIONAL INFORMATION		
Carbohydrate	12	g
Protein	7	g
Total fat	7	g
Cholesterol	1	mg
Sodium	207	mg
Fiber	4	g

Asparagus Frittata
From Italy • Pictured

• Wash the asparagus and remove the ends of the stalks. Thick stalks may be peeled thinner at the lower end. Cut into pieces about 1/2 inch (1 cm) long, then blanch in a large pot of boiling salted water for about 2 minutes; plunge into cold water to stop cooking. Peel the onions and chop fine.

• Heat 2 tablespoons oil in a large pan over medium heat. Add onions and sauté until translucent. Add asparagus and cook briefly. Remove the pan from the stove.

• In a large bowl, beat the eggs until foamy; season with salt and pepper. Stir in the asparagus mixture.

• Heat the remaining oil in the pan over medium heat. Pour in the egg mixture and spread it out in the pan. Let it cook over low heat for about 10 minutes.

• Slide the frittata onto a plate, then flip it back into the pan to cook on the other side. Continue cooking for 3 more minutes, or until set and golden brown. Makes 4 servings.

PER SERVING:	325 CALORIES	
NUTRITIONAL INFORMATION		
Carbohydrate	10	g
Protein	16	g
Total fat	24	g
Cholesterol	424	mg
Sodium	216	mg
Fiber	3	g

Pepper Omelet
From Spain • Easy to make

• Wash and seed the peppers, then cut them into small strips. Peel the onion and garlic and chop them fine. Wash the parsley. Remove the stems and chop the leaves fine.

• In a large bowl, whisk the eggs with the milk; season with salt and white pepper.

• Heat the oil in a large pan over medium heat. Add onion and garlic and sauté until translucent. Add pepper strips and parsley and sauté briefly.

• Stir the eggs, then pour over the pepper mixture, distributing egg mixture evenly in the pan. Let the omelet cook over low heat for about 10 minutes.

• Slide the omelet onto a plate, then flip it back into the pan to cook the other side. Cook the omelet for 3 minutes more, then serve hot or room temperature. Makes 4 servings.

PER SERVING:	325 CALORIES	
NUTRITIONAL INFORMATION		
Carbohydrate	14	g
Protein	15	g
Total fat	24	g
Cholesterol	425	mg
Sodium	215	mg
Fiber	3	g

Asparagus Frittata
1 1/8 lb (500 g) asparagus
salt
2 onions
4 tablespoons olive oil, divided
8 eggs
freshly ground white pepper

*Preparation time:
About 40 minutes*

Pepper Omelet
1 1/8 lb (500 g) red bell peppers
1 large onion
2 cloves garlic
1 bunch parsley
8 eggs
2 tablespoons milk
salt
freshly ground white pepper
1/4 cup (60 ml) olive oil

*Preparation time:
About 45 minutes*

For the Sweet Finale!

Desserts

Even though a meal in the Mediterranean countries almost never ends with the main dish, a sweet dessert is by no means obligatory. On normal weekdays, one is usually satisfied with a dish of mixed fresh fruit, a small choice of cheeses with grapes or olives, or even just a coffee or espresso. On holidays, it's an entirely different matter, for then a meal will extend over several hours and there will certainly be something sweet, in addition to cheese.

Sweet Variations

If you want to use other sweetening ingredients instead of white or brown sugar in these recipes, you can substitute honey or maple syrup in about three-quarters of the given quantity of sugar.

Planned Temptation

The desserts in this chapter are easy to make; however, some do take time. Many can be prepared several hours before the meal, making them ideal when entertaining guests. To make shopping easier, the following descriptions may help you with some unfamiliar ingredients.

• Anise-flavored liqueurs are found in all the Mediterranean countries. Whether you buy ouzo (from Greece), raki (from Turkey), or sambuca (from Italy) depends entirely on your personal tastes. You will find at least one of them in the larger liquor stores, or those specializing in foreign wines and liquors. In addition to using it in the dessert described, this liqueur tastes good in coffee or espresso.

• Almonds, the seeds of the almond tree, come from Asia, but they have long since spread over the entire Mediterranean area. They are divided into two categories: bitter and sweet. Bitter almonds contain hydrocyanic acid, which is destroyed when heated. The sale of bitter almonds is illegal in the United States. Sweet almonds are available blanched, raw, or toasted. If you purchase them raw, submerge the nuts in boiling water briefly. When cool enough to handle, pinch the nuts out of their skins. Before using, let them dry thoroughly, or let them dry overnight, spread out on a paper towel.

• Mascarpone is the best known Italian double cream cheese, and is used to make the popular tiramisu. Mascarpone is produced all over Italy, is firm and, except for the preparation of some pasta dishes, is used primarily for desserts. You can buy mascarpone in $^1/_2$- (225-g) or 1-pound (450-g) containers in specialty supermarkets, cheese stores, and Italian gourmet food shops.

• Orange-flower water gives many desserts a fine flavor. You can get it in foreign groceries, as well as gourmet shops and some pharmacies.

• Pine nuts ripen in the cones of pine trees. Since it is necessary to remove them from the individual chambers, the nuts are expensive. Pine nuts have a sweet-resiny taste, and contain as much fat as do other nuts. Therefore, they become rancid easily, and should only be bought in small quantities and used as quickly as possible. Always store leftover nuts in the refrigerator, in a tightly sealed container.

• Vanilla beans are the fruits of an orchid. The fine flavor is primarily contained in the tiny vanilla seeds inside the bean. To release the flavor, cut the bean in half lengthwise, then carefully scrape out the seeds with the point of a small knife. The bean pods also have some flavor. To make vanilla sugar, you can cut them into small pieces and store them in an airtight container with sugar. After about a week, the sugar has taken on the aroma of the vanilla, and can be used to flavor or decorate fruits or desserts.

Cheese Plate—Dessert for Gourmets

If you want to serve cheese as well as dessert, choose the varieties that would complement the dishes you have already served. If your menu is French or Italian, you should choose cheeses from these countries. With Greek, Spanish, and Turkish cheeses, the choice is rather narrow. Italian hard cheeses go best with Spanish dishes; food from Greece and Turkey can be paired with feta cheese and olives, or a hard cheese from Italy.

Almond Pine Nut Cookies

From Spain • Perfect for company

• Immerse the almonds in boiling water and let stand for about 10 minutes. Pour off the water, let cool somewhat, then press the almonds out of their skins. Rub the almonds thoroughly dry in a kitchen towel or let them dry spread out on paper towels overnight.

• Grind the almonds and confectioners' sugar, small portions at a time, in the food processor until very fine. Combine the almond-sugar mixture, orange-flower water, liqueur, almond extract, and eggs in a large mixing bowl and mix well.

• Preheat the oven to 350°F (180°C). Roll the almond mixture into walnut-size balls, then stick the pine nuts into the balls.

• Place the cookies on a greased baking sheet and bake in the hot oven for about 20 minutes, or until they are nicely browned. Makes about 35 cookies.

Orange Sorbet

From Italy • Refreshing

• Peel the oranges, removing as much of the white inner pith as possible. Cut the fruit into small pieces. Place orange pieces, confectioners' sugar, and about 1/2 cup (100 ml) water in the food processor; process to purée.

• Stir in liqueur and lemon juice, then pour into a shallow bowl and freeze for about 2 hours. Stir the mixture from time to time, so that it doesn't develop too many ice crystals.

• Place the frozen mixture into a mixing bowl and blend it with an electric mixer. Divide the mixture into 6 dessert dishes and freeze for another 2 hours, or pour the mixture back into the shallow bowl to freeze again.

• To serve, garnish each portion with orange slices and mint leaves. Almond Pine Nut Cookies are a nice accompaniment. Makes 6 servings.

Almond Pine Nut Cookies

3¹/₂ cups (400 g) almonds

1¹/₂ cups (175 g) confectioners' sugar

2 tablespoons orange-flower water or fresh orange juice

1 tablespoon orange liqueur

¹/₂ teaspoon almond extract

2 eggs

¹/₂ cup (100 g) pine nuts

Preparation time: About 1¹/₄ hours

Orange Sorbet

4 large oranges

²/₃ cup (80 g) confectioners' sugar

1 tablespoon orange liqueur or fresh orange juice

2 tablespoons fresh lemon juice

orange slices and mint leaves for garnish

Preparation time: About 15 minutes (plus about 4 hours for freezing)

PER SERVING (One Cookie): 113 CALORIES		
NUTRITIONAL INFORMATION		
Carbohydrate	7	g
Protein	4	g
Total fat	9	g
Cholesterol	12	mg
Sodium	5	mg
Fiber	2	g

PER SERVING: 86 CALORIES		
NUTRITIONAL INFORMATION		
Carbohydrate	22	g
Protein	1	g
Total fat	0	g
Cholesterol	0	mg
Sodium	0	mg
Fiber	2	g

Lemon Tart

For the dough:
2 cups (250 g) white flour
$1/3$ cup (70 g) sugar
$1/2$ cup (125 g) cold, unsalted
butter
$1/2$ lemon
$1/2$ teaspoon vanilla extract
1 egg yolk

For the filling:
4 eggs
1 egg yolk
1 cup (200 g) sugar
$2^1/2$ lemons
$1/2$ cup (130 ml) whipping
cream

For prebaking the pastry
shell:
Dried beans and parchment
paper

For dusting:
1 tablespoon confectioners'
sugar

Preparation time:
About $2^1/2$ hours (including
55 minutes for baking)

Lemon Tart
From France • Festive

• Combine flour, sugar, and butter, which has been cut into small pieces, in a large bowl. Wash and dry the lemon half. Grate the peel fine and add to the flour, along with the vanilla and egg yolk. Add about 1 tablespoon cold water to the mixture, and knead with your hands until it is a smooth, supple dough.

• Press the dough into an 11-inch springform pan so that it forms an edge about $3/4$ inch (2 cm) high; let dough rest in the refrigerator for about 1 hour.

• To make the filling, combine eggs, egg yolk, and sugar in a large bowl. Beat with an electric mixer until foamy. Wash the lemons in hot water and dry off. Finely grate the peel from $1^1/2$ lemons, adding to egg mixture. Squeeze juice from $2^1/2$ lemons into egg mixture, blending well. Beat whipping cream until stiff, then carefully fold it into the egg mixture, using a whisk.

• Preheat oven to 350°F (180°C). Place a piece of parchment paper on top of dough and cover parchment with dried beans.

• Bake the dough for about 10 minutes. Remove pan from oven to cool slightly, then remove the beans and the paper. Reduce oven temperature to 320°F (160°C).

• Pour the lemon filling into the crust, and bake the tart for about 45 minutes, or until the filling is firm.

• Let the tart cool in the pan. Preheat the broiler. Dust the tart with confectioners' sugar and place it under the broiler for about 1 minute, or until the tart is golden brown on top. Watch the tart while it is under the broiler so that it does not get too brown. Serve immediately. Makes 8 servings.

Variation:
The tart tastes good with orange instead of lemon. Use the juice of blood oranges and the peel of other oranges. You will need only $3/4$ cup (150 g) sugar for the filling.

PER SERVING:	471 CALORIES
NUTRITIONAL INFORMATION*	

Carbohydrate 61	g
Protein 8	g
Total fat 23	g
Cholesterol 212	mg
Sodium 92	mg
Fiber 1	g

*Refers to original recipe only.

Crème Caramel

From France • Classic

• Split the vanilla beans lengthwise; scrape seeds into a saucepan and add milk. Bring to a boil, then let stand for a while.

• Preheat the oven to 300°F (150°C). Melt 6 tablespoons sugar in a small saucepan over medium heat, and let it caramelize. Stir in about $1/2$ cup (100 ml) water, then immediately divide among six 5-ounce (150 ml) custard cups.

• In a large bowl, beat the eggs, egg yolks, and remaining sugar until foamy. Slowly add vanilla-milk to the egg mixture while stirring. Pour milk mixture into the prepared custard cups.

• Place the cups in a deep baking dish. Pour enough hot water into the baking dish to reach about two thirds of the way up the cups.

• Bake for about 1 hour. Do not allow the water to boil; if necessary add cold water.

• Allow the custard to cool. Unmold onto plates before serving. Makes 6 servings.

PER SERVING:	202 CALORIES	
NUTRITIONAL INFORMATION		
Carbohydrate	29	g
Protein	7	g
Total fat	7	g
Cholesterol	219	mg
Sodium	67	mg
Fiber	0	g

Semolina Halvah

From Turkey • Pictured

• Chop the walnuts fine. Melt the butter in a pan over medium heat. Add the nuts and toast, stirring, until they are lightly browned.

• Add the semolina and sugar, and cook, stirring, until the semolina is golden brown.

• Take the pan off the stove and mix in the milk. Stir in lemon peel and cloves, then return the pan to the stove. Cook the semolina over the lowest possible heat, stirring, until it is firm.

• Spoon semolina mixture into a bread pan that has been rinsed with cold water; spread the mixture smooth with a dampened spoon, then allow to cool.

• Let the Semolina Halvah cool for at least 2 hours. Loosen the halvah from the mold by running a knife around the edge; turn out onto a serving plate; dust with cinnamon, then slice. Drizzle lemon juice over top, if desired. Makes 6 servings.

March 2020 3.5/5 easy and I liked it. Bit of a mess though

PER SERVING:	328 CALORIES	
NUTRITIONAL INFORMATION		
Carbohydrate	29	g
Protein	6	g
Total fat	22	g
Cholesterol	51	mg
Sodium	109	mg
Fiber	1	g

Crème Caramel

2 vanilla beans
2 cups ($1/2$ l) milk
$3/4$ cup (170 g) sugar
2 eggs
4 egg yolks

*Preparation time:
About $1^1/2$ hours*

Semolina Halvah

$1/4$ cup (50 g) walnuts or almonds
$1/2$ cup (100 g) unsalted butter
2 cups (250 g) durum semolina flour
$1/2$ cup (125 g) sugar
$2^1/2$ cups (600 ml) milk
grated peel of 1 large lemon
pinch ground cloves
ground cinnamon for garnish
fresh lemon juice, optional

*Preparation time:
About 20 minutes
(plus 2 hours for cooling)*

For the cream puff dough:

1 cup (230 ml) water

$1/4$ cup (60 g) unsalted butter

1 tablespoon sugar

salt

$1^1/2$ cups (150 g) white flour

4 eggs

1 teaspoon baking powder

For the baking tins:

Shortening and flour

For the chocolate filling:

$2^1/2$ (1-oz/75-g) bittersweet chocolate squares

1 teaspoon instant coffee crystals

$1/2$ cup (100 g) heavy cream

1 teaspoon vanilla sugar (see page 83)

For the mascarpone filling:

1 lemon

1 vanilla bean

5 oz (150 g) mascarpone cheese

3 tablespoons heavy cream

2 tablespoons confectioners' sugar

For dusting:

Confectioners' sugar

Preparation time:

About $1^1/4$ hours

90

Cream Puff Duet
From France • Perfect for company

• To make the dough, combine water, butter, sugar, and a pinch of salt in a large saucepan over medium-high heat; bring to a boil. Remove pot from stove and add the flour all at once, stirring constantly.

• Place the pot on the stove again. Keep stirring the dough over the lowest heat until it comes together in a firm ball and pulls away from the sides of the pan.

• Place the dough in the large bowl of an electric mixer, and mix in 1 egg with the kneading hook. Let the dough cool to room temperature. Work in the remaining 3 eggs and baking powder.

• Preheat the oven to 350°F (180°C). Grease 2 baking sheets and sprinkle them with flour. Using a teaspoon, place small mounds of dough, 2 inches apart, on the sheets (there should be about 32 puffs).

• Bake the puffs about 35 minutes, or until they are golden brown. Do not open the oven for the first 20 minutes!

• Take the puffs out of the oven, and cool completely before cutting off the tops.

• To make chocolate filling, combine chocolate and coffee crystals in a large saucepan over low heat; melt chocolate, stirring occasionally. Whip the cream and vanilla sugar in a large mixing bowl until stiff. Mix half of the cream into the chocolate, then return chocolate-cream mixture to mixing bowl, folding gently into remaining whipped cream.

• For the mascarpone filling, wash the lemon in hot water and dry it. Grate the peel and squeeze the juice of half the lemon. Split the vanilla bean and scrape the seeds into a large bowl.

• Combine the mascarpone, lemon peel, about 2 tablespoons of lemon juice, cream, and the confectioners' sugar in the bowl with vanilla seeds; mix well.

• Fill half of the cream puffs with the chocolate mixture and half with the mascarpone mixture. Place the tops on the puffs, then sprinkle with sugar and serve immediately. Makes about 8 servings.

PER SERVING:	419 CALORIES
NUTRITIONAL INFORMATION	
Carbohydrate 29	g
Protein 8	g
Total fat 31	g
Cholesterol 190	mg
Sodium 186	mg
Fiber 1	g

Strawberries with Anise Cream

1¹/₃ lb (600 g) strawberries
¹/₄ cup (80 g) sugar, divided
1 cup (200 ml) heavy cream
3 tablespoons anise liqueur

For garnish:
Lemon balm leaves

Preparation time:
About 20 minutes

Pears in Red Wine

4 pears
3 cups (700 ml) dry red wine
1 cinnamon stick
2 or 3 cloves
1 vanilla bean
2 teaspoons vanilla sugar
(see page 83)
1 to 2 tablespoons fresh
lemon juice
¹/₂ cup (100 g) crème fraîche
or sour cream
1 tablespoon sugar
pinch ground cinnamon

Preparation time:
About 40 minutes
not including cooling time

92

Strawberries with Anise Cream
From Spain • Easy to make

• Wash the strawberries; remove the stems, and cut the berries in half. Mix strawberries in a large bowl with half the sugar, and let stand for about 10 minutes.

• In a large mixing bowl, beat the cream stiff with the remaining sugar and anise liqueur.

• Divide strawberries among 4 dessert dishes; cover with the cream, and serve garnished with lemon balm leaves. Makes 4 servings.

Variations:
This simple dessert can be adapted in a variety of ways: Use raspberries instead of strawberries, and cassis instead of anise liqueur; or use cherries with orange liqueur. Quartered fresh figs and grappa, or mixed berries with coffee liqueur are also good combinations.

PER SERVING:	387 CALORIES	
NUTRITIONAL INFORMATION*		
Carbohydrate .41	g
Protein 2	g
Total fat 23	g
Cholesterol .82	mg
Sodium 24	mg
Fiber 3	g

*Refers to original recipe only.

Pears in Red Wine
From Italy • Pictured

• Peel the pears and cut them in half.

• In a deep, 12-inch pan, combine the wine, cinnamon stick, cloves, and the split open vanilla bean. Add vanilla sugar and 1 tablespoon of lemon juice, then bring to a boil; let simmer for about 10 minutes.

• Lay the pears in the sauce cut side down, and let them cook for about 10 minutes over medium heat, turning once. Let the fruit cool in the sauce for at least 1 hour.

• In a small bowl, whisk the crème fraîche or sour cream with the sugar and ground cinnamon, then flavor to taste with lemon juice.

• Lift the pears from the sauce and divide them among 4 dessert dishes. Serve with the seasoned crème fraîche or sour cream. Makes 4 servings.

Variations:
The recipe is also good with peeled peaches.

PER SERVING:	304 CALORIES	
NUTRITIONAL INFORMATION*		
Carbohydrate .34	g
Protein 2	g
Total fat 7	g
Cholesterol .13	mg
Sodium 24	mg
Fiber 4	g

*Refers to original recipe only.

INDEX